MORAL INQUIRIES

A Kinship Classic

CONTEMPORARY PORTRAIT OF LEWIS GOMPERTZ

MORAL INQUIRIES

ON THE SITUATION OF MAN AND OF BRUTES

Lewis Gompertz

CENTAUR PRESS

FONTWELL   SUSSEX

This first paperback edition published 1992
by Centaur Press Ltd, Fontwell, Sussex BN18 0TA

© Centaur Press Ltd, 1992

British Library Cataloguing in Publication Data:
A catalogue record for this book is available
from the British Library

ISBN 0-900001-37-2

Typeset by
Willow-Type, East Dean, Sussex PO18 0JB
Printed and bound by
Antony Rowe Ltd., Chippenham, Wiltshire SN14 6QA

THE KINSHIP LIBRARY

"The cause of each and all of the evils that afflict the world is the same – the general lack of humanity, the lack of the knowledge that all sentient life is akin, and that he who injures a fellow being is in fact doing injury to himself."

Henry Salt: *Seventy Years Among Savages*

THE KINSHIP LIBRARY, to meet the growing demand from those concerned by the rising tide of human and animal suffering, offers work tracing the connection between our often lamentable behaviour toward each other, and our thoughtless and cruel exploitation of non-human species.

This aspect of humane education, given scant attention until recently, is becoming of major concern. The implications of Albert Schweitzer's perception that "until he extends the circle of his compassion to all living things, man will not himself find peace" are vital to any real growth in education. They explore the deepest level of the environmental conscience and have particular significance for students, teachers, and those most responsibly engaged in furthering the welfare and rights of animals.

The Kinship Library will present new books on the philosophy, politics and implications of those rights, and reissues of long unobtainable works of special merit, edited or introduced by modern scholars. The older reissues will be published as Kinship Classics.

Editorial advisors to The Kinship Library: Maureen Duffy; Audrey Eyton; George Hendrick; Charles Magel; Jan Morris; Tom Regan; Richard D. Ryder; Peter Singer; John Stockwell.

COVER: Naming the animals: from a fourth-century ivory.

PUBLISHER'S NOTE

Other Kinship Library titles published or pending include:

The Duty of Mercy by Humphry Primatt, edited and introduced by Richard D. Ryder.

All Heaven in a Rage by E.S. Turner.

The Universal Kinship by J. Howard Moore, introduced by Charles R. Magel.

On Abstinence from Animal Food by Joseph Ritson, introduced by Keith Tester.

Also an edited reissue of Edward Maitland's *Life of Anna Kingsford*; John Oswald's *The Cry of Nature*; E.W.B. Nicholson's *The Rights of an Animal*; William Youatt's *The Obligation and Extent of Humanity to Brutes*; Thomas Young's *Essay on Humanity to Animals*; Henry Salt's *Seventy Years Among Savages*; E.D. Buckner's *The Immortality of Animals*; J. Howard Moore's *The New Ethics*; selections from the works of J. Todd Ferrier, Thomas Tryon, Lord (Thomas) Erskine, Howard Williams, Francis Newman, J.A. Gleizes, J.F. Newton, Pierre Lotti, J.L. Joynes, Lady Florence Dixie, William Lambe, Jeremy Bentham, Ernest Bell and others. New books by modern philosophers and writers will be announced.

CONTENTS

CHAPTER I

OBSERVATIONS on the improvement society has undergone, and the prospect of its extending to the brute creation. Remarks on the state of the horses etc. which are employed by mankind, and some of their injuries described. Some of the cruelties on other animals adverted to. English and Portuguese manner of slaughtering oxen compared. Cruelty proceeds greatly from improper education. The difficulty of making rules for morality. View of the state of man and other animals, and their different qualities. Chief cause of the ascendency of man, and further improvements in society hinted. Instinct and reason; great sense and virtue of brutes. Anecdotes in evidence of the same. Similitude between man and other animals; deduction from the similitude. All difference of ideas and sensations arises from difference of organization. Difficulty of describing ideas. The notions some persons possess of a future state.   21

CHAPTER II

VIEW and comparison of man and other animals in a state of nature with that of civilization. Reflections on their sufferings. Further improvement hinted. That a great overstock of animals from increase of happiness may be impossible. The

CHAPTER V

CHAPTER VI

CHAPTER VII

CHAPTER VIII

CONTENTS

CHAPTER IX

CHAPTER X

CHAPTER XI

CHAPTER XII

CHAPTER XIII

FOREWORD
by Peter Singer

I FIRST read *Moral Inquiries on the Situation of Man and of Brutes* in 1973 in the British Museum Library, when I was working on my own *Animal Liberation*. In that book I argued that we ought to extend the principle of equal consideration of interests to all sentient creatures. Doing that, I argued, would mean that we ceased to eat them, or to treat them merely as tools for research. Despite my conviction that there were compelling moral reasons for the position I was defending, I was a little apprehensive to be putting so radical a position to my friends, colleagues and to the general public. It is easy to imagine, then, how astonished I was to find that Lewis Gompertz had been thinking along similar lines, 150 years earlier! I am therefore especially pleased that this book will once again be available to those who are not fortunate enough to have access to an outstanding library like that of the British Museum.

Gompertz was an authentic pioneering exponent of the set of ideas that, a century and a half later, have been taken up by the animal liberation movement. The text that follows shows this clearly. Consider, for instance, the axioms that he sets out in Chapter 4. It is enough if I here quote only *Axiom 5*:

> "That we should never admit of the propriety of the will or volition of one animal being the agent of another, unless we should perceive its own good to result from it, or that justice should require it."

To put such an axiom into practice would, at a stroke, end the use of animals as subjects of harmful research, and the use of animals for food. Indeed, Gompertz goes even further than ethical vegetarianism: he advocates a vegan diet. In Chapter 6, Gompertz argues that we exploit the cow when we make her produce more milk than is needed for her calf, and we exhaust the hen by making her lay more eggs. Consistently with his beliefs, Gompertz ate neither meat nor other animal products, and refused even to ride in a horse-drawn carriage - and in his day, the only other way to get around London was on foot.

Gompertz may well have been the first modern Western thinker to take so strong a stand in favour of equal consideration for animals, to argue for this position in a logical and philosophical manner, and to act accordingly. To say this is not, of course, to suggest that he had all the answers to the many dilemmas of living ethically in a world in which we must compete with animals for land to grow our food, and in which many animals prey upon each other. In such a short book, no-one could deal adequately with these very difficult ethical issues. Environmentalists, aware of the role of predators in maintaining ecological systems, will feel uneasy at Gompertz's apparent readiness, in Chapter 5, for whole species of carnivorous animals to become extinct (or live on vegetables!) so that their prey can live. Philosophers will wish that Gompertz had spent more time defending and explaining his "moral axioms" and the theorems that follow from them. All the same, we should remember that every thinker builds on the work of those who have gone before. No-one who reads the *Moral Inquiries* while bearing this in mind can fail to be impressed by Gompertz's effort to lay down a logical basis for an ethic that deals in a just and equal manner with nonhuman animals. His ideas remain well worth consideration today, although he had incomparably less to build on than those writing on this topic in the present century.

Gompertz's historical significance does not rest only on his writings. His eagerness to stop the needless suffering of the unjustly oppressed led him to play an active role in the development of the organization now known as the Royal Society for the Prevention of Cruelty to Animals. In 1824, the year in which Gompertz's *Moral Inquiries* appeared, a public meeting was held under the auspices of Richard Martin, MP, which led to the foundation of the Society for the Prevention of Cruelty to Animals. This society, which became "Royal" in 1840, with the support of the young Queen Victoria, was the mother of RSPCAs and SPCAs everywhere. William Wilberforce and Fowell Buxton, two leaders of the anti-slavery movement, were among its founders. Within two years, however, the newly-formed society was in serious trouble. Its first secretary, the Reverend Arthur Broome, was imprisoned because the society could not pay its debts. He was soon released, but he was not the right person for the position of secretary. He was succeeded by Gompertz, who served as a hard-working and energetic secretary for the next six years, setting the society on a firm footing. Then a dispute broke out within the society. (Those involved in the animal movement today may wryly acknowledge that in this respect too, little has changed.) According to Gompertz himself, he found that one of the most active members of the society was involved in behaviour "inimical to the institution" (tantalisingly, he gives no further details), but this individual was able to rally enough of his own supporters to force Gompertz out. Whether or not this was the cause, the manner in which Gompertz was forced out is sufficient, by today's standards, to discredit his opponents. A clergyman who was a member of the society claimed to detect in Gompertz's writings some doctrines held by the ancient Greek philosopher Pythagoras. He wrote to the committee that it was, in his view, essential that the society should propagate only Christian views. The committee duly resolved that the society should be exclusively Christian. Gompertz denied that his beliefs were Pythagorean; but he was Jewish, and so considered that the Committee's resolution was scarcely compatible with his continued membership. In any case, he very reasonably argued, the work of preventing cruelty to animals had nothing to do with religious sectarianism. Hence he resigned.

Gompertz's troubles with the Society for the Prevention of Cruelty to Animals did not deter him from working with animals. He founded the Animals' Friend Society in order to continue, as he wrote, "those operations which the Society for the Prevention of Cruelty to Animals, when united, so successfully performed." For some years Gompertz managed this new society with such zeal that it outstripped the one he had just quit. He also founded and edited the society's journal, called *The Animals' Friend, or the Progress of Humanity*. This appears to have been the world's first animal welfare periodical. Now Gompertz was free to speak his mind about the activities of some members of the Society that had forced him out. He wrote about how a pack of staghounds owned by Lord Suffield, a member of the SPCA, had pursued a stag for twenty-three miles at a pace that was, according to the *Morning Herald*, "almost unparalleled for its severity", but nevertheless "highly enjoyed by the sportsmen." The run so exhausted the stag that he died. Gompertz was also a fierce critic of the way sheep and cattle were beaten while being driven long distances to slaughter - and of the cruelty of the slaughter itself.

In 1846, ill health forced Gompertz to retire. The society he had founded went into decline and ultimately ceased to exist. Gompertz himself continued to write, publishing another significant, if less systematic, work, *Fragments in Defence of Animals*, in 1852. He also pursued his other chief interest as an inventor. A list of his inventions published in 1837 totalled thirty-eight. They have been described as "ingenious rather than practical", and included shot-proof ships, fortifications for reflecting cannon balls to the places from which they were fired, and a cure for apoplexy. (Perhaps this last was offered to those he attacked in his journal.) He did, however, achieve one striking success, with a device known as an "expanding chuck", which was attached to a lathe, and became very widely used. Many of his devices were attempts to improve the lives of animals.

Lewis Gompertz died on December 2, 1861. I feel sure that he died knowing that future generations would take his work further. All those who are working for animal liberation today can take pride in knowing that they are doing precisely that.

Sources:
For biographical information in this foreword I am indebted to E.S. Turner, *All Heaven in a Rage* (Centaur Press, 1992) and to the biography of Gompertz in *The Dictionary of National Biography*, edited by Sir Leslie Stephen and Sir Sidney Lee, Oxford University Press, 1917.

PREFACE

THOUGH, in presenting these few sheets to an enlightened public, I hope for their countenance and their indulgence, I am aware that many of the sentiments contained in them are too far different from those mostly entertained, to expect them to meet with immediate and general success: but were the sentiments the same as those of others, I might spare myself the pains of publishing them. My attempt has been chiefly to support the claim of the brute creation to the mercy of man: as far as I have in reason attained my object, I trust on meeting with such candour from my readers (if I should have any) as may be expected from the present time, and which the importance of the subjects treated on demands.

In any production, where the Author's attention has been particularly devoted to his subject, relating to affairs that concern all mankind, and where their opinions have been previously formed, it is a matter of doubt whether its meeting with general approbation speaks much in favour of the correctness of the contents, or general censure much against it; universal applause being, according to Seneca, "two thirds of a scandal." It is, however, one thing to reason well, and another to entice others to devote sufficient attention to us to perceive that we have really done so, this requiring the address which few possess; and whatever truth the arguments may contain, we must not think that it will generally appear, unless we can introduce them so as to promise a reward to those who may bestow their time and thoughts on them, and without which it is not to be expected that any opinion, at variance with the sentiments of persons who are to judge of them, can be approved of; as, should it be better or worse than those of others, it is plain that in neither case will it be the same, and may in consequence be rejected. It is to be lamented that many works of real merit fail from this cause. But where the opinions coincide with the ideas of the majority, they in consequence become popular; because, if the Author's thoughts are the same as those of the Reader, it is a truism that the Reader's thoughts must be the same as those of the Author, and who, if possessed of sufficient skill to show them in a more clear point of view than he can himself, need not then despair of receiving his patronage, both being partisans of the same cause. I however do not mean to assert, that the sentiments contained here are generally in opposition to those of most other persons, though in many cases, and particularly where the brute creation is the subject, they are certainly different, and perhaps sometimes wrong, however unconscious I may be of it myself.

I hope also that in other cases I shall not be taxed with presumption in attempting to discuss matters which seem beyond the powers of more able investigation than mine; but it is to be observed that persons are frequently deterred from entering into subjects that cannot be brought to actual demonstration, because they would not be contented with any thing less, whatever presumptive evidence they might be able to draw from their inquiries; but to me it appears that where the former cannot be attained, we should be thankful if we can reach the latter. Others are prevented from attempting any thing difficult, because they take the whole difficulty in their minds at once, and are disheartened by the disparity appearing between that and their own powers. Their manner of viewing such subjects resembles that of a person who attempts to walk in a dark road without being accustomed to it: he endeavours to look too far, and perceives nothing but darkness before him; but by perseverance the pupil becomes dilated, the sight improved, and the understanding taught that it will suffice to see but one step at once; this being gained, the next is as clear as the first was before, and by degrees the one mass of darkness becomes divided among a multitude of spaces, each possessing sufficient light to proceed by. I will not however waste any further time with comparisons, as comparisons are not arguments, but will yield to the impulse of my wishes to proceed to my business with alacrity, with interest, and with hopes; and feeling convinced that my cause is good, I will venture boldly on it, knowing that, if unsuccessful, I shall still feel gratified that my intention was good.

CHAPTER I

Observations on the improvement society has undergone, and the prospect of its extending to the brute creation. Remarks on the state of the horses, etc. which are employed by mankind, and some of their injuries described. Some of the cruelties on other animals adverted to. English and Portuguese manner of slaughtering oxen compared. Cruelty proceeds greatly from improper education. The difficulty of making rules for morality. View of the state of man and other animals, and their different qualities. Chief cause of the ascendency of man, and further improvements in society hinted. Instinct and reason; great sense and virtue of brutes. Anecdotes in evidence of the same. Similitude between man and other animals; deduction from the similitude. All difference of ideas and sensations arises from difference of organization. Difficulty of describing ideas. The notion some persons possess of a future state.

"While man explains, 'See all things for my use!'
'See man for mine!' replies a pamper'd goose."
                                        Pope's Essay on Man.

Various have been the attempts of the present day towards the amelioration of society, and fortunate have been the efforts of genius and of virtue in increasing the happiness and in improving the character of man. But in this age of intelligence, the energy of which is less diverted by war, the morals of mankind less injured by its baneful influence, it is indeed to be expected that much more will be done. That time may, we trust, not be far distant, when all men will treat each other as brothers; when each individual will

21

participate in the good of his neighbour, and add sympathy instead of reproach to his sufferings and failings, of whatever nature they may happen to be. Even the brute creation have not been entirely forgotten: and it is to be hoped that the results of the exertions of Lord Erskine and Mr. Martin will prove to be the foundation of a general system of humanity, extensive in its objects, and happy in its effects.

But as this subject has been less investigated than those immediately concerning mankind, I hope that a few words which I have here to address to the public will not be entirely disregarded. I must begin by observing that there are two circumstances to which our inattention to those things we ought to know is in most cases to be attributed: the first is *want* of information, and the second is *too much* information, so that, in becoming familiar to the thing, our senses cease to be affected by it.

The dreadful situation of the brute creation, particularly of those which have been domesticated, claims our strictest attention. Let every mind capable of reflection, direct it for a moment to that of the horse and the ass, by whose exertions we (in the present state of things) derive so much advantage; and let their cases be examined by a judgement unbiassed by habit. We are indeed so accustomed to see their excruciating sufferings, that they fail of exciting the attention even of the benevolent, who concur in the idea that a horse was created to be whipped on its almost bare skin, simply to compel it to perform the labour that the purpose or caprice of his master may require; and in doing which so many persons take delight, to the utmost of what the nature of the animal can support.

Let the general characters of our coachmen, carmen, postillions, etc., be considered; men who have not had the advantage of a good education, and who are mostly chosen as possessing good and healthy constitutions; little acquainted with painful sensations, and much less disposed to experience any for the sufferings of their cattle; let us reflect on the natural desire of most men for domineering over others. Let it be remembered that these men, from their want of power and their inability of exercising any tyranny over their fellow-creatures, give unrestrained scope to their barbarity on their cattle, which it seems they justly indeed consider as their slaves, and whom, from ignorance and love of cruelty, they press to such a degree, as to render them incapable of yielding the profit which a milder treatment would ensure. And it is to *these* men, then, that *these* creatures, seemingly possessed of feelings very similar to our own, are completely given up during their whole lives of above twenty years, when the very idea of our being at the mercy of the former for an instant would be dreaded!

The elegant appearance of some of our horses, and the health they seem to possess, naturally incline us to suppose them to be in a state of enjoyment. But how many of these elegant animals are destroyed monthly, and daily, by our stage-coachmen, postillions, etc., who only calculate on their own profits! Besides, it must be recollected that it requires very great sufferings, and time, to effect much change in the figure of an animal in the prime of life; and a view of their whole lives will also lead to a very different impression. When the young horse is first receiving his education, he is immediately taught to be suspicious and fearful by the torture it commences with, and by the different mutilations he is then subjected to; the very possession of their tails and ears has been deemed too great an indulgence; and sometimes the mere amputation of the former will not suffice, the stump must also undergo the operation of nicking. This consists in making several cuts across the inside of the stump, which is then kept strained towards the back of the animal, so as to prevent it from ever afterwards lying in its natural position[1]. They are then, after suffering still greater mutilations, *broken-in*, as it is termed, in a manner the severity of which is of course according to the disposition of their tutors; to the difficulty with which they understand the signs of man, whose language they are unacquainted with; and to the aversion they very naturally and justly evince at being enslaved and ill-treated. They are however at last, by dint of punishment, made subservient to our use. They have then two thick irons placed in their mouths, by which they are controlled: these are occasionally pulled and jerked by their drunken drivers with their whole force, notwithstanding that one of them acts by a lever to increase its power. The sides of their mouths and their tongues are said frequently to get between these two irons, and to be wounded by them, as is sometimes indicated by their bleeding. They are then incessantly flogged, spurred, and over-exerted, to set off their master's equipage, for the amusement of his servants, or some other unworthy purpose, till they lose a great part of their strength and beauty, and are afterwards sold to some stageman, hackney-coachman, etc., by whom, besides being half-starved, they are worse treated because their strength is less, till they become unfit for any purpose but a dust-cart for a scavenger, or perhaps for a dealer in horse-flesh, who takes care to get his last penny out of them, and who frequently finds it to his interest to finish by working them to death.

This is the unexaggerated state of the generality of the horses of *humane* Englishmen. There are even very many of them suffering still more, and which are continually to be seen in our hackney-coaches, etc., adding lameness to their

---

[1] The former operation, termed *docking*, is performed by a kind of shears, after which the tail is cauterized, or burnt with a hot iron; various machines and pungent applications being used after nicking, as if solely to increase the torture of the animal; each operation at times producing locked jaw, mortification, and death.

other calamities; and which, after having had their eyes cut out by strokes of the whip, are, by fear of chastisement, compelled to go quickly, and in the greatest dread, over ground that they cannot see, and without giving any proof of their relying on the guidance of their drivers.

It is strange that persons who would shudder at the idea of even *seeing* a human being flogged, think nothing of witnessing or even inflicting themselves the like punishment on dumb animals. They seem to think it of no importance, because they are used to it; and truly do they suffer every day and continually, what we should think a severe trial for half an hour.

Only let the number of lashes and blows of some of those which are the worst off be computed. Suppose we assume upon an average three per minute (as we seldom meet with a bad hackney-coach or cart-horse, or ass, without witnessing at least one), that is 180 per hour; and if on an average we estimate six hours work per day, that makes 1080 per day. These are mostly inflicted at the moment when they produce the severest effect; that is, when fatigue has increased their sensibility, when any accident has caused a false step, or when they happen to be alarmed, circumstances which are laid hold of by their drivers as faults requiring correction, being glad to find a plea for exercising their power just at the time when they can with the least trouble give the animal the most pain. They generally make an excuse for ill-treating their horses, by saying that they are obliged to do so on account of the heaviness of the roads, or from their having the day before been driven an immoderate distance, and therefore require goading, or to their having at other times done more; and construe every loss of strength from fatigue or disease, into perverseness, without considering that the strength of an animal is not always the same. This spirit of proportioning the magnitude of the punishment to the incapability of bearing it, is manifest in the treatment which asses receive: these being much smaller and weaker, are commonly even more ill-used; though it is evident that the smaller an animal is, generally the less should be the blows to produce the same effect; as a blow that would kill a mouse, would scarcely be felt if inflicted on a man.

It is besides to be considered, that the means used to make them perform work that is beyond their strength, are those which render them still less capable to accomplish it; though they may produce temporary and supernatural exertion. How can it ever be supposed, if the powers of an animal should be unequal to the task while it is sold and well, that it should be more able when it is half-killed? It being a fact that every blow deprives it of some of its strength and spirits; also that the muscles which move the limbs of an animal are disposed all over its body; so that every bruise or hurt inflicted upon it, must produce some *lameness* and inability in the limbs - of the truth of which every person must some time have had experience on himself; and besides which, it being actually proved, that in countries where asses are better treated, they are much stronger and more active than they are here. It would however seem unnecessary to enlarge on the subject, as any one who only takes a walk in our public streets and roads will there see much more than I can describe, and will, if possessed of any thought, be shocked at the wanton barbarity continually practised on dumb animals, particularly when the roads are heavy, and when frost and snow present additional hardships for them to struggle with. What prison offers a more faithful picture of wretchedness, than is here continually presented before our eyes? Though it must be confessed, that since the New Hackney Coach Act has passed, considerable improvement has taken place. But is it not a shame for Englishmen, who boast so much of their humanity, that (as is well known) they treat their horses and asses with much more cruelty than their neighbours do on the continent? In Holland, though they are likewise at times ill-treated, they are frequently encouraged to work by the kindest caresses; and postillions there, when they find their horses much fatigued, will generally refuse to proceed with them for any bribe; the carmen's whips there are mere play-things to those used in England, nothing like a whip of eleven or twelve feet long being seen there. It is not only worthy of observation, how much delight some persons take in inflicting misery on brutes, as is evinced by the pleasures of the chase, etc., but it is also almost as much to be remarked, how many of those persons who do not actually take pleasure in it, can be entirely indifferent to the happiness of those animals they have taken in their charge; and who would cause them to feel pleasure or pain, according to which they should themselves derive the most profit. They would grieve to see some of the varnish scratched off their carriage, yet mindless whether the skins of their horses were lacerated or not, as nature repairs the one injury without expense, but not the other; and they would without the least violation of their conscience use their animals as they would do their tools, without the slightest regard to their feelings, their wants, and their desires. It is true that they treat them well when they find their account in it; but ill, where they think ill-treatment answers best. Their wants are disregarded, their desires curbed or destroyed, and their bodies cut and disfigured, when it suits those persons' purpose so to do.

It is usually observed that it does horses good to give them exercise, and that it is therefore just to employ them; and it is as often asked why they should live in idleness, while men are obliged to work, not taking into account the difference between employment undertaken by a person voluntarily for his own benefit, and at his own management of himself, with regard to the little periods of rest, acceleration, and retardation, in the exercise; and such kind of labour as what an animal is obliged to perform, at the command of another, continually scourged, scared, and ill-treated; and being destitute of the advantage of speech, that he may, when unable to work well, say BY WHAT AILMENT HE IS PREVENTED. How little must those persons know of the animal economy, who are ignorant of the fact, that in order to make the greatest exertions, we ought to be in good spirits, and happy, and that pain greatly reduces our powers of labour; but still the love of cruelty seems to blind men to their own interest, and cause them to prefer inflicting misery to receiving gain.

It needs but little power of rhetoric to prove, that it is highly culpable in man to torture the brute creation for amusement: but strange it would seem this self-evident principle is not only openly violated by men, whose rank in life has denied them the benefit of good education or leisure for reflection, but also by those with whom neither expense nor trouble has been spared towards the formation of their intellectual powers, even in their most abstracted recesses; and who in other respects delight in the application of their abilities towards every thing that is good and meritorious. It is to be lamented that even philosophers frequently forget themselves on this subject, and relate, with the greatest indifference, the numerous barbarous and merciless experiments they have performed on the suffering and innocent brutes, even on those which show affection for them; and then coldly make their observations and calculations on every different form in which the agony produced by them manifests itself. But this they do for the advancement of science and expect much praise from their meritorious exertions; forgetting that science should be subservient to the welfare of man and other animals, and ought not to be pursued merely through emulation, nor even for the sensual gratification the mind derives from them, at the expense of justice, the destruction of the happiness of others, and the production of their misery - as pleasure and pain are the only things of importance. But those who may plead, that they perform their experiments for the advantage of mankind, at the sacrifice of brutes, I must refer to the sequel, where we hope that the invalidity of the excuse will be evident.

But besides those acts of cruelty we have alluded to, and which are continually before the eyes of every one, what numerous barbarities are dumb animals caused to endure from man! These, though seldom under our immediate observation, it would far exceed our limits to particularize. But those cruelties we have just treated on, being once admitted as such, others must be acknowledged in consequence, though self-evident besides.

Who can dispute the inhumanity of the sport of hunting, of pursuing a poor defenceless creature for mere amusement, till it becomes exhausted by terror and fatigue, and of then causing it to be torn to pieces by a pack of dogs? From what kind of instruction can men, and even women, imbibe such principles as these? How is it possible they can justify it? And what can their pleasure in it consist of? Is it not solely in the agony they produce to the animal? They will pretend that it is not, and try to make us believe so too, that it is merely in the pursuit. But what is the object of their pursuit? Is there any other than to torment and destroy? If it were merely in the speed, racing would be equally pleasing to them. Let those who love this amusement fancy themselves in the situation of their game, running before their hounds; and let them then state the ecstasies they have experienced, and applaud themselves for their bravery.

Even dogs, man's favourite animals, are commonly sacrificed to his mere sport, for which purpose they are caused to fight and to mangle each other, till his entertainment becomes complete - exhibitions of that disgraceful description being given in rooms appropriated to the purpose, in different parts of London and Westminster: and cats still more frequently suffer from the barbarity of many persons in whose possession they happen to fall, and which may be daily seen starving about the areas of different houses, where they are ill-treated by the servants, tormented by the children, and disregarded by the families who inhabit them.

Those cruelties caused by the refinements in cookery are too notorious, and too often adverted to by different authors, to escape the notice of the public; and the enormity of the crime of boiling living lobsters and other shell-fish, and of whipping pigs to death, must be apparent to every one; as must also the practices of skinning living eels, and of hooking the heads and tails of flat-fish together in a bent position; and even the practice of drovers, of cutting the ends of the tails of oxen, when they take off the tuft of hair, and which is claimed by themselves, or by the salesman, as perquisites, the oxen being afterwards driven about with their tails bleeding, and deprived of their hair. Even in the manner of slaughtering animals how much unnecessary pain are they put to! When by following the Portuguese method of dividing the spinal marrow in the neck, so much might apparently be saved! One of the modes pursued here with oxen is represented to be that of striking them several times on their heads, with a heavy and slender-headed hammer, sometimes unskilfully, till it is completely buried in the skull, the hammer being then taken out of the wound and a stick introduced in its place, and further pressed into the brains, which are stirred about with this stick, when the agony of the beast becomes apparent by the groans it utters.

With regard to those animals termed vermin, as rats, wasps, beetles etc., it seems that many persons consider themselves as licensed to practice every kind of cruelty upon them, and to destroy them in the most efficacious manner, however barbarous it may be; as by burning, poisoning, and the like. This is called self-defence; but in which case we prescribe very severe punishments for very slight offences, and are frequently beforehand with them.

It seems that the crime of cruelty proceeds greatly from

improper education. Subjects of moral inquiry are too often chased from the attention of youth, from a false idea that they are mere chimeras too difficult to enter into, that they only serve to confound us and to lead us into disputes, which never come to a conclusion; that they cause us to fall into eccentricities, and unfit us for all the offices of life, and at last drive us into downright madness.

Forbid it that we should give assent to such tenets as these! That we should suffer for one moment our reason to be veiled by such delusions! But on the contrary let us hold fast every idea, and cherish every glimmering of such kind of knowledge, as that, which shall enable us to distinguish between *right* and *wrong*, what is due to one individual, what to another.

In order to lead us into just conclusions, there are almost an infinite number of subjects to be considered; but what are most essential I think may be confined to these:

First. The nature and degree of the sensations, the construction and constitution of man and other animals.

Secondly. What are the most rational ideas regarding prior and future states of existence.

Thirdly. The nature of personal identity.

A knowledge of which subjects being gained, it will then appear, what right man has to exert his power over other animals, to slaughter them for food, to enslave them to perform his labour, and to punish them for his pleasure.

But from the very cradle do we imbibe our first notions of things, and by instinct do we imitate the actions of those persons with whom we are most intimately connected. So strongly indeed are we impressed with the ideas which have been instilled into us in our early years, that at the most remote stage of life we remember keenly events that have occurred in our infancy, and forget those which have taken place the very hour that is past. We admit as self-evident truths, principles we have never examined, and often attempt to overturn what is most strictly correct, because in contradiction to those very opinions we have by habit formed on uninvestigated and unsolid grounds.

This is really the fact with the bulk of mankind, and even with many of those who possess the best talents on subjects to which their attention happens to have been directed; but who, on having their early adopted notions in the least doubted or even questioned, would startle at the rashness of him who should dare to attack such firmly rooted conceptions: thus disturbing the thread of the systems they have formed; and which on being disturbed would involve them in difficulties and perplexities, inimical to the regular order of their lives, to their own sentiments, and even to the great infringement of their happiness. All this must be admitted: but *truth* must be admitted also; and whether the result of our inquiry turn out as we wish, or whether it should lead us into conclusions hostile to our well-being, *truth* is still *truth*, and must be revered notwithstanding.

But before I enter into this subject, I must aver that I expect only to be opposed by such arguments as may be supported on bare reason, and not to any article of faith or revelation; my aim being to discover truth by our reasoning faculties. These constitute the ground on which I build, and on this ground must the fabric fall if it be erroneous. But those who may wish for a proof of the crime of cruelty to animals founded on Scriptural researches, I refer to Mr. Primatt's work on the subject, though the privilege of slaughtering them or using them for our necessity is not there contested. I have been taxed with inconsistency, because I admit certain laws and privileges, and exclude others; and because my ideas differ from the opinions generally entertained, it has been expected for them to embrace every perfection, while the imperfections of a contrary course are entirely overlooked.

All systems in which it is attempted to classify and distinguish matters from each other, form a kind of boundary, imaginary or real, between what objects it places in one class and what in another: these lines have, in several instances, been made with great discernment by different philosophers: but whether they have related to moral actions, or to other scientific pursuit, they have never been perfectly defined, and in spite of all endeavours they will in some degree infringe on each other.

The naturalist tells us what animals belong to one species, what to another, what beings may be called animals, and what vegetables: and the chemist is as systematic in his science; he calls several different substances metals, others earths, salts, etc. These distinctions, however proper they seem, are acknowledged to be in some degree arbitrary, and are founded on some certain properties of them being similar to each other; and though two substances of different species may in some respects resemble one another, less than two others of the same, they are still, for the sake of order, ranked together, having certain properties in common.

The science of morality is also in some degree arbitrary: and even the different axioms on which its justice is established, have perhaps been more disputed than the elements of any other science. However, let every person choose his own axioms, etc., by which he reasons, and he can then only be taxed in two ways; first, on the propriety of his axioms, etc.; and secondly, as to his arguments being in harmony with them. But whether or not they be at variance with those of other persons, he can never be brought to task for that, on the ground of inconsistency. I shall therefore, in the sequel, lay down some of my own, and will then state my ideas depending on them; and though chiefly relating to dumb animals, also, in many instances, applying to mankind. We will, however, first take a short view of the state of man and other animals, in order to judge what they own to each other, and what privileges they both may claim. It is proper to consider the situation of man and of brutes, in a natural and also in a domestic state, respecting the quality and degree of their sensations, the several evils brutes are subject to in a natural state, as well as in a domestic state. It will also be necessary to show the general injustice of mankind, in forcing them to act against their will to perform his labour, and in slaughtering them for food; a comparison then of their separate cases of happiness and misery will tend to the results sought for. And further, it seems requisite to make some surmises on the state of all animals, prior to this life, and beyond it.

That we may take a just view of the nature and state of man, we must first consider him in himself, totally unconnected with his kind, without any other ideas than those he would acquire simply by his own means, and without the assistance of any contrivance to enable him to collect those of others, or even by which he might recollect his own. What a degraded state of humanity would this be! It appears to me that it might even be inferior to that of most other animals; and that, notwithstanding the boasted superiority enjoyed by man, his real sense may even be less than that of many of them, though I do not assert it to be so. But happily for him, and unhappily for other animals, man, by associating with his kind, acquires the power of *increasing* his knowledge, by which, added to his being furnished with hands, he is enabled to improve his own situation, and to depress that of other animals; it being a known fact, that wherever mankind dwells, other animals show less sagacity and perform less for themselves than where they are alone. It is true that to man belongs the honour of the *invention* of language, but which, though more fruitful in its results than the inventions of other animals, may still not have required so much intellect to produce as many of theirs. By the single advantage of *speech*, and its modification *writing*, man may be said to possess his knowledge in a store-house, which he is continually obliged to apply to in consulting with his kind, and with his own past ideas: much of the knowledge of the whole species from ages back becomes thus concentrated in each individual, in addition to his own small share. This invention besides gives such advantages, and puts the productions of the world so much in the power of man, that other inventions rise in consequence: so that there is scarcely an insect, a vegetable, or a material, but what become applied in various ways to improve the condition of man, and which appears even now to be in its infancy, by the very great superiority possessed by every other age over the preceding one.

What a difference exists in the progress of most of the arts and sciences, in chemistry, in surgery, in music, in practical mechanics, etc., and by what rapid strides have they advanced! It might thence be inferred, unless much is forgotten, that the species of man has not been long created; and in favour of which hypothesis, we are also furnished with the known fact, that among the different strata which have been examined, are to be discovered almost unequivocal signs of several distinct races of animals, no human bones being found in the very newest deposits, and every formation possessing peculiar organic remains.

It seems reasonable to expect that the state of man will still be much higher, and that it will rise by degrees to the greatest perfection of which his nature is susceptible: but that he will then be prevented from gaining more knowledge, by his capacity being stocked. If this state should ever arrive, he will probably then lose nearly all his knowledge together; because his thoughts may become so divided, that he may be unable to fix them on any particular thing, one of which may so hide another as to put it nearly out of sight; the attention will it seems then sicken at the multitude of subjects, and general ignorance may then be the consequence.

Yet however the state of man may be above that of other animals, if the superiority be owing to his being differently situated, we must not dazzle ourselves by gazing on the brilliancy of the situation, but learn how to estimate their true qualities only; though the situation gives the one the powers to act, and denies it to the other.

It has been generally, but not always, the custom of naturalists to degrade the powers of dumb animals into mere instinct, and not to allow them reason; and on the other hand to elevate the qualities of man, by entirely disavowing the power of instinct in man, giving him the use of reason alone. It appears to me, that there *is* such a quality as instinct; by which I understand a desire to do any thing without knowing why, or without having the object in view which it is to reach. I am of opinion that both reason and instinct act in man and also in brutes; and I will even grant that the proportion of reason to instinct is greater in man than in other animals; but that the latter possess a great portion of reason would it seems be absurd to dispute.

When for instance an insect lays her eggs in a hole, and then collects a number of other kinds of insects, and places them in the hole with her eggs, for her young ones to eat when they come to be hatched, and dies herself before that time; this appears to be dictated by instinct: because otherwise the insect must possess knowledge without experience, and must even be a prophet, to know that young ones will come from the eggs. When a bird builds a nest, or a bee honeycomb, though there appears to be instinct in these actions also, in either case the instinct can only apply to the motive, or rather to the desire, they entertain in doing it: as certainly all the difficult operations necessary in the construction of a nest or a honeycomb, executed with such skill, and under such a variety of circumstances, relative to the place where they build, to the shape of their work, to the different kind of materials they find, etc.; all this requires reason in them, to adapt their means to such various circumstances, and reason -innate, as they seem to act without instruction. And without tools, with bad materials, and even without hands, do they perform work which would (as I have seen observed) almost defy the imitation of the best workman, with good tools, with materials collected from every part of the world, seven years apprenticeship and practice, and aided by the inventions of many ages.

The state of infancy in man agrees with the idea of his real sense being probably less than that of most other animals; though I do not assert it to be so. But here we see him, however, perhaps with his intellects not come to perfection, destitute of acquired knowledge or experience, with less judgement in acting than a colt, though it seems doubtful whether maturity can boast of more real sense than infancy; it is almost certain that the mind in infancy makes more progress in its first years than it does afterwards, which circumstance would seem to indicate greater sense instead of less, but still less than that of a colt, for the time being; though the mind of a child may possess more of a certain quality, leading to improvement, than that of a colt, but which improvement is also owing to the advantageous circumstances whereby he is surrounded. I do not, however, assert either that the mind of infancy is really superior to that of manhood, on account of its aptitude of acquiring knowledge being greater, because possibly this may be owing to the capacity being more vacant. It is also evident that there is not any other animal apt to run into such extreme follies as man occasionally does. And while human beings believe in witches, in the necessity of inquisitions, in various kinds of superstition; while they take the veil in convents, and cause their offsprings to sacrifice themselves in that manner; while they tattoo their skins, make holes in their ears and their noses to put ornaments in, and cramp their feet in iron shoes to prevent their growing; brutes are not subject to any thing in lieu of these absurdities which is half so ridiculous.

There seems, however, to be a great difference in the sense of different animals; and one example of the highest kind is continually before us - in spiders, the general habits of which are well known; the beautiful construction of their webs, and in taking their prey. It is to be observed that in summer there are seldom to be seen any living prey in their webs, as they mostly destroy such insects immediately; but in the autumn there are generally a great number of insects hanging in bags of cobweb seemingly dead, and even apparently half decayed; but on these bags being carefully taken off they immediately emanate, and fly away from their miserable confinement, where they had been placed by the spider to be preserved for a considerable time. Besides this, the extreme animation they show when they take their prey, when they fight, or when their webs are touched, which they shake to frighten away their enemy, and many other of their actions, all show the strength of their intellects, though in this case joined to a ferocious disposition.

But besides this, and the example of what animals, such as birds, bees, ants, beavers, etc., perform in their natural state, it is well known that they can receive some instruction from man. Birds learn to sing real music according to our own scales, correctly, with good intonation, good emphasis, and in good time: they learn in a small degree to talk, and to understand what they say too; and though they may not mean the same thing in what they repeat as we do, what does that signify? They mean something else specific, as they say different things upon different occasions, sometimes even the very thing which is right, and done with design. Do not monkeys and dogs acquire the art of dancing? It is even reported that horses have been taught writing, or of marking different figures together to compose the product. Now if this were even done by signs from its master, must not the sagacity of the animal be very great to comprehend them? And how much of their natural abilities do they retain in a domestic state! What a nice observation, and what a retentive memory must a dog possess, who finds his way home for many miles on the first time of his being taken to another place! This does not seem to be done by means of their scent; as dogs which cannot follow their game for a mile by scent, can also find their way; and moreover, they do not give any signs of being guided by it. We must therefore own that in *this*, they show a keener observation and a more retentive memory than we should do, who would be obliged to ask our way home. We have heard of cats having found their way back after having been taken away in a bag, where they could not see. But this does not argue the less reason, as having trusted to their scent; because whether done by sight, by scent, or by any other faculty, it must be by a great number of sights or scents, etc., following each other in a certain order of succession, noticed and wonderfully retained by the animals in retracing their way; added to the great degree of judgement they evince, what superior *virtues* are they embellished with! And though many of them are extremely vicious, how few are there whose vices are not in a great measure mixed with good feelings!

From them mankind may learn maternal, filial, conjugal, and in some cases paternal affection. They also show great friendship at times for each other. Heroic and superior courage is another quality that they strikingly display; though this can only be ranked as a virtue, when well directed, and when it does not proceed from ignorance or insensibility, which of course are not in themselves virtues, though they may both frequently be necessary to screen the mind from danger.

From them we may also learn to be candid. When a dog or a cat gives signs of attachment to their master, we are generally almost certain that it is real; they love his society, they regard him with looks unmixed with envy, soothe him when he is dejected, make no impertinent and injudicious comparisons between his lot and theirs, and show the utmost gratitude for whatever trifles they receive from him; not that kind of gratitude which is connected with the idea of obligation, and a desire to free themselves from the weight of it, by giving him some good in return; but such gratitude as what only endears the animal and the master to each other, and which urges a dog to yield his life to serve his master. Even from the ass may we take examples of one of the first qualities of the mind, in which the greatest philosophers can scarcely vie with him; consisting in the exercise of that resigned Christian-like and even Stoic-like fortitude, that would have done honour to Zeno himself, continually evinced through a long life of almost incessant torture and trouble, inflicted on him by man, who only derides his sufferings, and wonders at his stupidity, that he himself has caused by injuring his head with blows, and by other ill-treatment. The great contempt this animal is held in, is even apparent by the way in which he is spoken of, the very name having been changed into *slang* language for another term.

From some birds we may learn real constancy in conjugal affection, though in most instances their contracts only last for one season, but how strict do they keep this! They have no laws, no parchments, no parsons, no fear to injuring their characters, not even their own words to break in being untrue to each other: but their own virtue is their laws, their parchments, their parsons, and their reputation; their *deeds* are their *acts*, their *acts* - their *deeds*: and from their own breasts do they honestly tear down to line the beds of their legitimate offspring.

I have lately witnessed a curious circumstance in evidence of the sagacity of blackbirds. I observed a male blackbird flying about in a extreme state of agitation; and on my going to discover the cause of it, the bird retreated from me as I followed it, till it stopped at a nest containing a female bird sitting upon her eggs, near which there was a cat: in consequence of this I removed the cat, and the bird became quiet. After that, whenever the cat was about the place, the blackbird would come near my window, and would in the same manner direct me to some spot where the cat happened to be stationed. I have also heard of a male blackbird having attacked a cat which had caught the female: they generally sit at some distance from their nests, and seem to give the female notice of danger.

The strength of affection in porcupines will appear in the following anecdote. A person having kept two porcupines, had his attention one morning arrested, by one of them running round a particular spot in great distress; when it was discovered that the other porcupine was lying dead on that spot.

Bitches have been known upon losing their young to refuse food, till they had discovered where they were buried.

Three anecdotes have lately appeared in the newspapers worthy of recollection. One concerning two goats which had met each other in a narrow path between two precipices, where there was not room to turn or to pass, when one of them lay down, and suffered the other to walk over it. The second related to a horse, which having been hurt by a nail in being shod, had gone back to the farrier, and shown his foot to him. And the third alluded to a shepherd's dog having jumped into the water to another dog in distress, floating on a piece of ice, and of the former having brought him safe to the shore. Cats which have been ill, have submitted to painful operations from those to whom they were attached, without showing the least signs of anger; but on the contrary with great tokens of gratitude, and on return of the complaint would come in a plaintive manner seemingly to have it repeated.

I would now fain ask, if all this does not show reason and virtue? And if it is possible to be the result of bare instinct?

Are they not furnished with most feelings similar to our own? They indisputably evince in an eminent degree most of the same passions. Things which affect us, generally seem to affect them in the same way; and at least the following sensations and passions are common to both, viz. hunger, desire, emulation, love of liberty, playfulness, fear, shame, anger, and many other affections though they are destitute of the power of laughter. But little occasion have they to exercise such a faculty!

They are both born of two parents; many of them breathing the same air in nearly the same manner, robbing it of part of its oxygen, and impregnating the remainder with carbon; the blood of each being distributed through the body of arteries, propelled by the action of the heart, nourished by the oxygen, and conveyed back again by the veins.

Both performing muscular motion by the action of the brain on the nerves, by the nerves on the muscles, and by the muscles on the bones.

Both feeling pleasure and pain by the connection of the nerves with the brain.

Both nourished by similar food, digesting it by similar organs and menstrums, converting part of it into chyle, and by similar lacteals, secreting it to circulate with the blood, from whence, by means of the different glands, the body becomes furnished by the several fluids, for the same purposes in each.

It would, in fact, be presumption in me to attempt to dwell on the striking similitude in the structure and operations of the bodies of all animals, which may be collected from many able physiologists, who have explored the mechanism of both, and from whence it will appear that the analogy is great, and the difference small, between many of them and ourselves.

But the matter does not stop here. What results from all this similitude of construction? Undoubtedly similitude of sensation. Two pieces of similar mechanism always produce the same effects: and it moreover appears plain to me, that all the sensations and the reasoning faculties of man himself, are produced by the mechanism or organization of his body joined to his particular identity, which will be hereafter treated on; and also to external causes; and that after death neither man nor brutes can ever exist in any state without another body, and in which condition they have no recollections of this life, the mechanism being destroyed from whence their knowledge proceeded: it being the fact, that not any sensation or action can exist without some alteration of the mechanism, and that every change produces different sensations, and even different judgements in the same person. For instance, illness, health, youth, age, intoxication, breathing of gaseous oxide of azot (which subjects persons to violent laughing); all these produce different affections of the mind and the judgement. Under one excitement we are energetic, and under another inactive and indolent, timid or bold, happy or miserable, virtuous or vicious, just as the parts of our bodies are disposed.

It will perhaps here be said that monkeys, so nearly resembling man in form, have very different minds. But it must be recollected that the want of speech and of communication, may prevent their powers being called into action; and that they do not seem to differ so much from a savage. It may further be said, that deaf and dumb persons possess good abilities, and can transact business as others do. This certainly shows that cultivated man is very different from a monkey, although without speech; but we must not lose sight of the fact that monkeys are taken from their natural state, by a set of beings who, though greatly resembling them, may be so far different as to be incapable of instructing them by any tokens that they can well understand; and their feelings may still very much resemble those of man, but not sufficiently so for them to enter well into the habits of cultivated manners. Even between different individuals of the human kind, one possesses very different sorts of feelings and sentiments to another; so much so, that it is frequently impossible for the one to convey his ideas to the other. And what does this proceed from but because, in order for one person to understand another, he must have the same sensations himself, and have been accustomed to a similar mode of life?

For instance, it would be impossible for one man to represent to another the sensations of giddiness or bitterness, if he had never had actual experience of them. It is also to be observed, that there is a considerable difference in the anatomy of man and of monkeys, in parts which are within the research of naturalists; and most likely still more in those that are beyond it. The elementary feelings, such as bodily pain, fear, love of liberty, etc., seem, however, to be very similar notwithstanding; and there is, it seems, little doubt that, were the entire mechanism the same, the qualities would also be the same.

In the very playing of two kittens may be discovered many of the chief passions of man: they have a meaning in every motion, each of which is a rehearsal of what they are afterwards to perform. At times they act the taking of their prey; at other times their manner of making love, or of fighting, in which they make use of ambuscades, of feints, and of guarded positions; in these they fortify themselves, and perform many other manoeuvres. The playing of two children, however engaging it may be, is certainly vague in comparison to this.

Most persons seem to be of opinion, that the qualities of the mind do not proceed from mechanism, that the mind acts independently of the body; and also that the mind having once acquired ideas, would still possess them, were it afterwards to animate another body: and in proof of this they advance, rather reasonably, that some insects, etc., are born with so much sense (for instance a bee, which begins to make a honeycomb as soon as it is in the form of a bee), as to indicate that they had previously existed in some other state, where they had gained their knowledge; and it is also observed by them, that as man is continually learning something till death, his acquirements would be thrown away, unless he should retain them in an after state. However, if this be true, the similitude between man and brutes will still appear, both being then subject to the same circumstances. But however reasonable this theory may appear, I think that the reverse is more so; because our memory fails us even in this life - not only from old age or disease, but even sometimes in youth and in health: therefore why should it last after the destruction of the body? Besides this, if the mind were continually gaining ideas in every state, the capacity would become overcharged; every idea requiring some time to act in, and not to be obstructed by other ideas at the same time: consequently the more of them there should be, the less number of times would each have to come into action; and at last they would be so numerous as to become almost useless to any kind of body that we can conceive.

CHAPTER II

View and comparison of man and other animals in a state of nature
with that of civilization. Reflections on their sufferings. Further
improvement hinted. That a great overstock of animals from
increase of happiness may be impossible. The reason why man was
made superior to other animals. Effects of habit.

—————

RESPECTING the state of savage or uncultivated life, man and
other animals appear to be very similarly circumstanced;
both of them being miserably subject to almost every evil,
destitute of the means of palliating them; living in the
continual apprehension of immediate starvation, of destruction by their enemies, which swarm around them; of receiving dreadful injuries from the revengeful and malicious
feelings of their associates, uncontrolled by laws or by education, and acting as their strength alone dictates; without
proper shelter from the inclemencies of the weather; without
proper attention and medical or surgical aid in sickness;
destitute frequently of fire, of candle-light, and (in man) also
of clothing; without amusements or occupations, excepting
a few, the chief of which are immediately necessary for their
existence, and subject to all the ill consequences arising from
the want of them.

It is true that the savage state has been painted in very
bright colours; but it is to be recollected that these descrip-
tions are rather to be considered as designs than copies. It is
not by such slight observation as that which any traveller can
have opportunity of making, that intimate acquaintance can
be obtained of the life of a savage man, or of any other animal.

Can it be supposed for a moment that a number of improvements in laws, in institutions and in inventions, are to no purpose? Far from that seems to be the case. But without viewing all the different scenes of nature, or the *present* improved state of it, as so many modifications of enjoyment, and that this world is that place of milk and honey which some are wont to believe, I yet trust in the goodness and power of the Almighty. And though I cannot conceive how any person can shut his eyes to the general state of misery throughout the universe, I still think that it is for a wise purpose; that the evils of life, which could not properly be otherwise, will in the course of time be rectified, and the exquisite pleasures for which we are formed will be enjoyed in our progeny: also that we may ourselves become the inhabitants of the improved world, or of some other world improved in a like manner; and that even if the different species of all the present animals should become extinct, as indicated by what we have observed of the different bones in the several strata, the discoveries of the present time may enrich the future, unless every trace of them should be destroyed at once.

This appears the best way of accounting for the present generally sad state of most animals, consistently with the greatness and goodness of the Supreme Being. But let it be asked of those who think they can perceive much of his goodness in the *present* happiness of his creatures - where do they find the examples? Is it in a hackney coach-horse, in a rat, in a flying-fish, or in a man? It has been remarked by a great author, that God is infinitely good, because his goodness is infinitely extended, all animals enjoying some of it. But on the other hand, they all feel some evil, consequently the evil is also infinite: therefore from *this* argument, which appears faulty, we might it seems as well erroneously infer that God was infinitely bad. Besides, goodness infinitely extended is of little importance, unless the share to each individual be moderately great; and even then it would not be infinite goodness, unless the degree or quality of it were infinitely great also, which is a subject beyond our conception, though infinite goodness be an attribute of the Deity. But could it only appear that the generality of animals felt more pleasure than pain, it would render the argument of expected improvement less necessary.

Delightful representations of animated nature have indeed been made by the best authors, which I hope I shall be pardoned in dissenting from, and confess that though I am not blind to there being much enjoyment, the different evils of all animals, and of all classes of mankind, strike me with the most force. Those authors construe almost all things into so many tokens of happiness. If they look at a drop of water through a microscope, and see a multitude of animalcula swimming about, they seem to conclude that they must all be in a state of pleasure; not judging by analogy, that for one whose motions are the effect of happy sensation, there may be several which are struggling for food, from disease, and other such causes; that even the very fluid they inhabit is disputed by larger animals, who are continually destroying them and giving them the agonies of death after a very short life, whether it be of pleasure or of pain, and thereby embittering the draught of the thinking part of mankind. The different actions and cries indeed of all creatures, are adverted to as enlivening scenes of happiness; not noticing how many of them, which to the uninformed may appear to proceed from enjoyment, are in fact produced by fear, anger, pain, and the like; and which close observation will frequently discover them to be. How are the weak and sickly males oppressed by the strong and healthy ones, crossed in their amours, deprived of their food, injured in their bodies, and at last driven to end their lives in solitary places!

It is strange that philosophers first show how one animal supports itself by destroying another, and then enter into discussions on the *apparent* admirable order of things in their present state. But though this may be a necessary contrivance, and the only way in which life can be supported, it can never be a beautiful one, in our short sights, notwithstanding that something worse might be, were this not the case.

In order to admire the goodness of God with the greatest force, we should endeavour to reach in imagination the improved state of the world, which it seems probable will be effected in the course of time. What may not be expected from the genius of man, which appears to gain fresh powers from every new idea that he gains from his fellows, and fresh means from all the inventions which the united efforts of the whole species bring forth? It is the extent of combination which chiefly raises man above brutes; and to combination are we to look to mature the views of Providence in forming society, and in regulating the affairs of life. Then will every animal within the reach of man feel the effects of his power, by his *increase of happiness* instead of his *misery*; and then only may man boast of his being lord of the creation, for which he *will be* fitted. But then man *will be* what man *is not now*, educated in the manner which further refinement shall point out; when for almost every vice and every disease there shall be known a remedy; and when almost every evil will find, in some discovery, a cure. The surprising effect of combination may be learned from the ingenious and philanthropic Mr. Robert Owen, who shows by what means a number of persons appear to be rendered comfortable, and for less expense than one individual can in the ordinary manner.

But a question naturally arises here, not only relating to the advantages of combination, but also to every other improvement which might take place in the condition of man; and this is, whether or not the world would soon become overstocked by an great increase of happiness, food, etc., being effected? Also, whether there is not some other limit fixed by nature to the increase of population, than that which proceeds from the distress caused by an overflow? But that there may be some other limit, seemingly can be maintained without absurdity; and this will be explained in a corollary to Theorem 1, in the sequel.

In this happy state of improvement, then, man will discover why many other animals have been put in his power; that, having established his own welfare, improved his understanding and his disposition, he will become the father of all within his reach. *His power* will supply *their want* of it; he will have learnt the art of improving the knowledge of other animals, and of gaining their affections; and will derive assistance from them in return, without coercion, the natural tendency in most animals of becoming attached to man, being strikingly apparent, when not too much ill-treated. But whether he gains their affection or not, he will never make use of his power to their injury, to increase his own good, unless it be to prevent their doing mischief, and unless they give evident signs that they would.

But it is here to be remarked, that in such an improved state of society, man will apparently have but little occasion for the assistance of other animals: divers intentions will, it seems, generally supply their place, and even do better than animal labour: man, then becoming truly religious, will glory in superintending the works of his Maker, which he has enstrusted to him: as a faithful servant, he will then not deny to what he now calls the *meanest reptile*, his protection, and own it to be his *brother*, resembling himself in construction, and created with similar care by the Supreme Being. Still in this age of imperfection we disdain to direct our attention to that on which God hath bestowed his. But this seems to be still the age of infancy, and baby-like do we cry, This is all made for me! The land and the ocean abound with myriads of animated beings of admirable construction only for me to play with, to torment, and to destroy. This is what we are taught. Besides, might is right; and it cannot be supposed that the head of the creation was not intended to derive any advantage from the inferior parts, far less to be their slave: and for what use can they possibly be, but for the good of me?

But the man of the improved age will speak thus: Whichever way I direct my observation, I see the power and goodness of my Maker. What multitudes of animals do I behold! All variations of myself! Every one appearing to be the work of the same inimitable Artist! All created with powers to enjoy their own existence; though *none* so great as myself, and most of them incapable of establishing and maintaining their own well-being. But I, being the head, I will direct them; this is my office: and how much do I consider myself honoured, to second these important works which God hath made! It was partly for this that I was formed superior; otherwise I should have been unfit for the charge. This will constitute much of my amusement, instead of hunting, shooting, bull-baiting, etc., but which I had used to think that I spent my time innocently. Still, might is right, when judgement is might, though not when might is judgement.

But to return to our subject. Though brutes suffer much in a natural state, they seem to endure much more when in our power; and in the former state all appearing to mix much enjoyment with their troubles, particularly the horse and the ass, which (as is well known) when wild, form societies, and appoint sentinels to warn them of danger, find their *food* beneath their feet, their *shelter* in the warmth of the climate, and make use of their strength with which they are endowed, in travelling about for fresh food, in defending themselves, and in escaping from their enemies; in this state the ass is known to be as active and spirited, as he is here dull and dejected.

It has frequently been advanced, that habit renders animals callous to blows; and it is I think a far too prevalent opinion, that where custom is present it cures almost every evil, though that it frequently lightens their weight would be in vain to dispute.

The force of custom or habit is even proverbial; and accordingly we take advantage of the magnified representation in which we have been pleased to paint its effects, to veil our eyes from the sufferings of others, of mankind as well as of brutes; and whatever be their lots, if they suffer from over exertion, from being flogged, from exposure in danger, from want, from cold, from heat, etc., we lull our imagination with the idea that they do not feel those evils: custom we say is second nature. It would seem, however, that the effects of custom are much more limited, and that its operations are partly as follows:

That almost every action which an animal performs, or what it is caused to endure, not only relates to the action itself, but leaves some effect on the constitution for a long while afterwards, and, when not too violent, generally renders it more able to perform or suffer the action again; this by dint of repetition becomes much better performed, and with more ease. An animal, then, having for a length of time practised and borne certain actions, becomes at last considerably altered by them; and it seems not unlikely that this alteration may affect the offsprings; which again continuing in practice of the same actions as the parent, further increase their own powers in those actions, and in turn communicate some improvement to the next race; and so for the rest, till the quality of the animal succeeding it becomes as much altered as its nature will allow; but which change at last, falls far short of the extent that we assign to it at its first step. It is then to be recollected, that when the force of the action exceeds a certain limit, a retrograde effect takes place; inability then resulting instead of improvement. But when death itself is caused by the evil, the force of habit is shown with *increased* though *false* powers, in its destroying the weak and leaving the strong. See Mr. John Hunt's *Anatomical Reflections on the*

Form of Animals; and his allusion to the fact, that more soldiers die in a first campaign than in succeeding ones - the infirm, being unable to bear the hardships, dying, and leaving only the robust: from whence it is erroneously supposed that habit has effected such surprising changes in rendering the soldiers hardy. But it is true that habit will sooner make nearly a whole nation hardy than one particular individual.

We shall now, in order to lead to just comparisons between mankind and brutes, and between man and man, offer a few observations on some of the most general cases of the present state of society, and point out the cause of many of the evils attached to it.

CHAPTER III

Short view of civilized society. Difference of rank. Observations on the different classes of society. Cause of difference of rank. Ill-treatment of Women. General injustice and spirit of rivalry in mankind. Happiness not attached to virtue.

———

In a state of nature, the cases of different individuals of the human species being little affected by variety in their modes of life, the chief difference in their degrees of happiness and of their sense consists in the difference of their constitutions; and where this is similar, they may generally be considered as one kind. But man, as in this age he is, may be said to be composed of more varieties and genera than any other species whatever.

This may easily be conceived, when it is recollected that the character of the man of the present age, not only depends (as in the former case) on the primeval variations of the complicated mechanism of his parts, these appearing to form his constitution, and even the disposition of his mind, but also on a multiplicity of different circumstances whereby he is surrounded; and that these two cases must be multiplied together, to produce the number of characters he exhibits, thus producing, it may almost be said, an endless variety, without being very fastidious in the gradations.

As soon as civilization and association begin to appear, petty warfare accompanies them; each individual generally striving to raise himself, by trampling on his companions, and to grasp more of the common bounty or Providence than comes to his share: still the more any one succeeds in his attempts, though it is to the injury of the rest, the higher is the degree of his rank estimated; which quality making no appearance but by comparison, and being improvable by depressing others as well as by raising himself, the former being the easiest, is unfortunately that which is most resorted to: from whence proceed many of the evils of life, and the humiliation and mortification of one part of a community, for the glory and comfort of the other.

But as the objects of desire in man are continually varying according to the circumstances by which he is stimulated, the nature of those qualities by which rank is measured must change with them. Hence follow the strange and opposite ways wherein different countries and different individuals guide their steps in pursuit of happiness, and in elevating the rank they are held in by their associates; the respect they promise to themselves being the goal by which they are infatuated, and this more or less alluring the whole mass of mankind in the struggle; yet though their paths be different, their interests are the same: while each conceives the reward of his labour to proceed from the object where his labour has been bestowed, where his eyes have been directed, and where his mind has been biassed: and many, through false and deluded judgements, though they succeed in their progress, miss what they had in view, finding only a misrepresentation fraught with more evil than good. And while some few slowly and laboriously attain the reality, thousands who had flattered themselves with their speed, at last perceive that they were descending, fall themselves, and cause others to stumble over them.

It is certain that the attainment of reputation and fame, on the one part, and the avoiding of disgrace and infamy, on the other, produce some of the strongest and most general feelings of human nature, whether the objects be good or bad. Some in pursuit of fame place their glory in bloodshed and oppression; even the virtuous themselves sometimes feel additional desire in doing good, from the approbation they expect to receive. A Chinese shows his rank by allowing his nails to grow, so as to render useless that noble piece of mechanism the hand, which others glory in having good use of. One man aims at riches, another at science and accomplishments, the chief object of each being generally the same; namely, that of gaining fame and respect, according to their different notions of what fame and respect are most due to; though the man who pursues riches calls his own exertions necessary labour, and those of the other merely amusement; while the man of different occupations retaliates, and pronounces the object of riches to be beneath his notice - both of them being thus apt to undervalue each other.

In the commencement of society, courage and strength forming the chief requisites for obtaining the necessaries of that state, they were the chief standards in the measurement of rank; and as these qualities were found useful, they became themselves to be the objects of admiration. But as property began to be acquired by their means, besides its own value it stood as the indications of courage and strength, the display of property being then found a cheaper exhibition of courage and strength, than any other mode of bringing them into notice; which also uniting with it the power of obtaining assistance in danger, for pay, and of affording aid to others when in want of it, the accumulation and display of profuse property became the greatest objects of human ambition, and the possession of it estimated beyond the more valuable gifts of personal endowments, even of health itself, which also enables persons to afford aid to others in need.

But as property began to grow unequal, those possessed of it began to find that it yielded them further advantages; and on account of its affording opportunity to men to associate with each other, and to produce a degree of intellectual improvement, the man of property soon discovered the way of duping the rest, and of deriving his further wealth from the source of their labour instead of his own: Thus the disparity became continually greater; and after some had monopolized almost the whole of the property, they made laws to protect it, regardless of what degree of severity they were fraught with.

The abject state of the poor did not however rest here, but in proportion as it grew defenceless, it became the more depressed; till at last the poor were degraded into the mere slaves of the rich; who, finding that they could satisfy their wants without labour, began to look upon labour as disgraceful, and as a sign of poverty: they therefore cast it off altogether; they imposed on themselves the task of idleness instead, and on this they rested their dignity. But in attempting to impose on others, they have worked their own evil; and have in many cases become the subjects of sloth, inability and *ennui*: they not only destroy their own happiness, but draw others into the snare, and grow perhaps in many instances worse off than the poor whom they oppress, whom they consign to over-exertion, to want, and to exposure to all kinds of dangers and troubles. And while the poor furnish and produce almost every thing that is useful and valuable, they are despised and underrated by the rich, who, frequently, do but little else or wish otherwise than to consume the fruits of the industry, of the genius, and of the labour of the poor, who for want of time and necessaries are obliged even to neglect their own persons, and those arts and accomplishments which would render them agreeable to others; thus seeming as if meritedly to incur the contempt they are held in even to their faces, by their being forced to bow and cringe to those who are termed their superiors, and not even permitted to be seated in their presence.

The difference of rank is by some held to be unavoidable and necessary: but whether this be the case, or not, is not our present object to inquire into, this being chiefly intended as a comparison of the state of man with that of brutes; and to point out that from the difference of rank, and from the sources of contention, there arises a great degree of evil to all classes of men, which in justice to man must not be overlooked in the comparison between him and brutes.

It is also true that, whatever class of mankind we examine, we find many distinct troubles attached to it, exclusively of such kind of unhappiness as does not relate to any peculiar mode of life, or what may affect particular individuals; life itself *beginning* and *ending* in suffering, and, as it seems, generally continuing during its course also with a balance of suffering, caused the different difficulties, disappointments, and other evils to which it is subject, where he is continually exchanging some perfections in his body, for an infirmity; and losing the possession of his friends or of other things essential to his happiness; with the constant anxiety of an eternal futurity presented to his sight, and being entirely ignorant of what may be his fate in it. Some being doomed to practise a variety of hazardous employments; others to over exertion of their strength: Some to irksome sedentary occupations, or to constant and difficult manual operations and straining of attention: many allotted to spend their lives underground in mines, to breathe foul air: and numbers being compelled to follow trades which expose them to all inclemencies of weather, and to other circumstances that lay foundations for the most inveterate diseases. Among the most common evils are the ill treatment met with by apprentices from their masters, and women from their husbands, who frequently from neglect of education, and favoured by the laws of their own sex, exercise their authority as they think suitable to the dignity of themselves; and mistake their superiority of strength, which was given to them partly for the purpose of defending their wives and labouring for them - for a privilege from God to exercise their tyranny towards them. It is known that generally the less society is civilized, the worse is the treatment of women. But it is strange in such a country as England, that women should still be degraded and ill treated, and confined to lower occupations than men are; that they should meet with less lenity in courts of justice, as well as more illiberality in private life; that the law should ever have subjected women to commit the crime of murder on their husbands to be burned alive for it, while men for a similar crime were only sentenced to be executed in the common way. But men made the laws; and as they thought it very terrible to be killed by their wives, they deemed it better to burn them alive, than to submit to such a danger. They also further took care to frame such laws as should give themselves the advantage; and to allot the most virtuous and best half of mankind, that was meant as the emblems of human perfection, to offices for which they seem never to have been intended, to the injury of their true qualities, and to the sentiments they inspire.

Respecting the evils which high rank gives birth to, they are indeed numerous, where men, from being provided with the necessaries of life, instead of having that stimulus to exertion which in others proceeds from the prospect of some future good resulting from their actions, are prevented by the laws of fashion from exerting their powers, or from *stooping* to any kind of labour or business - thus becoming enervated from inaction, justly discontented with themselves - envied and despised by the world. They have their game without the chase, without honour, and with the ill-will of their kind. They are subject to many of the worst evils of life, without commiseration or relief, through a false idea that they must be happy because they have money. It is true that there is sometimes sufficient energy in their constitutions to rouse them into action for the benefit and improvement of society: but it is not less a fact, that they do not generally meet with the same consideration or encouragement as others who work for themselves and their families. The former must be contented if they can do good, and still have their exertions, and their time, treated lightly by the world: though in the present state of things, it is to some of this class that the world are to look, for improvements in morals, for discoveries, and for perfecting the arts of life.

But the various classes of society, though frequently possessed of charitable feelings for each other - owing to the difference of their pursuits, generally keep apart, and consider those differently situated as far inferior to themselves. Even soldiers and sailors have a natural antipathy to one another. Nobility, gentry, commercial men, and mechanics, think the employment of each other insignificant; mutually ridicule them, and overlook the value of their separate abilities. The rich, while they admire and covet the works of the poor, despise the makers, and place the most ignorant of the poor in the same view with the most able and ingenious workman to whom they are debtors; and because their minds are less informed on some subjects, which they have attended to themselves, than those of the former, they designate them with the title of ignorant, and treat them according to the honour they have thus conferred on them.

The poor, on the other hand, ridicule the inability or the awkward and effeminate manner generally attached to the rich in performing the most common and necessary actions of life, where some exertion of strength is required; and are frequently more apt to laugh at the wig or long gown of a parson or counsellor, than to be awed into veneration and obedience by them. They in their turn think that persons of higher rank than themselves know nothing, and do nothing; and confound with the thoughtless, those who devote themselves to the promoting the good of the world, which these consider as the business belonging to them, in return for their consumption of the fruits of the labour of the poor; as whoever possesses or acquires a fortune, whereby he lives plentifully, and does not in some way return the benefit to the world, must be aware, that though his actions are honest, they are only so according to a law which is not sufficiently extensive to embrace much, and he lives without infringing the rules of his agreement.

But his conscience tells him that the gifts of Providence were made for all alike, and it is not by any other act that he can have a just claim to the fruits of the labour of his fellows, than by giving them the fruits of his own, if he can, in return: any other kind of property tendered instead, would then be illegitimate, and would be robbing one part of society to pay another, which is the cause of the great disparity of property now existing; though this is said to be an advantage to the poor, by their being employed by the rich in consequence: but it is evident that they would prefer to be their own masters; and that if the rich could not afford to purchase more than they could themselves, the poor would be richer for it, it being plain that if one man drinks all the cream, the rest will have nothing but skimmed milk.

A spirit of rivalry seems to run through society, even existing between male and female; and while the former cause the latter to have inferior educations and occupations to those of themselves, they despise them for the want of that knowledge and that honour of which they have deprived them; and even prevent their having any share in the formation of the laws of society, which would receive such essential improvements from a mixture of the superior refinement of the mind of the female, added to that kind of judgement which is possessed by the male.

But the contention for superiority goes still further; it travels from sect to sect, from country to country, and at last stretches from man to brute, spreading every kind of mischief in its progress, and giving rise to those feelings which authorize man to appropriate every other creature to his own purpose, and sanctioned by a false conception of their insignificance. Never must we admit of the propriety of this - which will shortly be discussed between Y and Z. But as to the ills themselves, it is natural on beholding an effect to inquire into the cause: let us then yield to nature, and soon shall we discover part of the source of many of the ills we have treated on. We have before attached blame to education; and here we must renew the charge: as, notwithstanding that ambition may be the medium through which evils pass, education is the power that propels them.

The instructors of youth should first try to excite the feelings of humanity, and to guide the power of reason in the minds of their pupils; and not venture to place in their hands the powerful engine of ambition, till they are fit for the trust. The first years of instruction should be spent in encouraging and counteracting the propensities of the child. The deformity of injustice and cruelty should be strongly impressed on him, particularly in such actions as those which he might wish to perform, as of boasting of any advantages over his companions, of robbing birds of their young, or of sticking pins in cockchafers; the mortification, the distress, and the pain these acts produce, should be faithfully delineated to him.

Principles of benevolence being established, we should proceed to moral questions, in which we should reject their assent to what we advance till they are conscious of its justice. And above all we should be careful not to rouse their emulation, but when the object was virtuous.

Still, fearing that it may appear as if I had been actuated to give too strong a representation to the sufferings of brutes, in comparison with those of mankind, I have yet to observe, that I not only perceive, but am deeply impressed with a knowledge of the magnitude of the different evils which are inseparable from human nature, and am even of opinion that they are generally treated too lightly by some of our best authors. It further seems to me that it is a very injurious, though a prevalent mode of reasoning, where virtue and happiness are invariably linked together, and vice and misery. So far from assenting to this doctrine am I, that virtue and happiness are viewed by me as being almost incompatible with each other.

This appears indeed a shrewd and harsh method of stopping the mouth of complaint, and of forcing back the virus of a suffering object, which he had attempted to relieve himself of, upon his own wounds. It has frequently been asserted by authors, though it seems with a good intention, that "no man is miserable but by his own fault." But what good purpose this slander on the unfortunate can accomplish, is difficult to discover, as is also how the idea can appear correct. And even in cases in which it *may be* his *fault,* what is *fault* but *infirmity*? And though sometimes a proper hint may lead a patient to perform his own cure, how many cases are there beyond the depth which human skill can fathom, and where any rough attempt would only be adding useless torment to a hopeless malady! Far otherwise must the disarrangements of the human frame be treated! These should not be touched but with the greatest care and study, and every effort made with delicacy and strict observance of the effect produced; and frequently requiring only soothing medicines, administered with discretion; though in certain cases of crime a different course is necessary.

Contrary to the opinion that happiness and virtue are always attached together, it seems to me that not any action can be truly meritorious but that which *injures* the performer. *He* must be bad indeed who would not do good if it cost him nothing. It may be said that the virtue consists in receiving pleasure from doing good: this is the reward the performer receives, and may in many cases be more than an equivalent for what it cost him. Thus far this theory seems just. But when it is considered that the same virtue which leads persons to derive pleasure from doing good, also leads them to feel pain when they perceive suffering in other beings that they cannot prevent; even moderate virtue is not so soon satisfied with itself. Those who reflect, must inevitably suffer much uneasiness; and little need they exert their skill to discover the difficulty of the situation in which they are placed in life. Without instruction, without a hand-post, and without a guide, are they left to pursue their course, through a path full of asperities and dangers, and where they cannot make a step without doing mischief. They however lay the task on themselves of going on right, and for want of knowledge are in perpetual hesitation and dilemma. It is true, if we could all be good boys and trust in our tutors, we should proceed more smoothly; but the restlessness of our own judgements teaches us differently: it either imposes the sufferance of severe privations, and the performance of difficult duties, or the poignant and humiliating reflections of self-reproach, and self-insignificance, besides the still greater evils frequently caused by the combat produced in the mind by the contemplation of two different actions, both of which appear to be duties, and being at variance with each other.

But independently of this, how many troubles are irrelative to either virtue or vice! *Pain* is *pain*, and *pleasure* is *pleasure*, in spite of any thing to the contrary; and the same of desires and aversions, which may be curbed but not quelled. And whether pain proceeds from a redundant or diseased sensibility, or from want of judgement to ward it off, it is great cruelty to add reproach to it instead of relief, though possibly in a few cases this may be necessary; but the reproach of its being caused entirely by our own fault, will notwithstanding be unjust. Even judgement itself lead us to discover many ills which in ignorance lie concealed; and it appears that we may safely pronounce happiness to shed its favours on the giddy and the thoughtless more than on the virtuous.

But lest this should appear as an encouragement to vice, it is particularly to be understood, that to a good person good actions will be most profitable, though the state of being good may in itself generally be unprofitable: and while the virtuous feel concern and anxiety for all, the profligate see the drooping and the dissolution of their nearest relatives with indifference, or with cheering hopes of their own gain.

Besides, if nature should have endowed one person with something that supports him in difficulties, and have denied it to another; let him not bask too much in the idea that he bears courageously what others shrink at, but recollect that true suffering consists in the effect produced on the mind, and if he can *bear more* it may be because he *feels less*.

For instance, the bodily pain persons undergo from the same cause, varies according to the state of their minds; and the greatest bodily sufferings have been partly neutralised by pleasure introduced in the mind by some other cause. Children will receive hurts in play without minding them, which at another time they would have cried for: and the greatest punishments of martyrdom have been gloried in and overpowered by stronger affections of the mind.

However, in pursuance of our subject it is to be observed, that the object of morality is to produce pleasure in others, and to prevent their feeling pain, or being injured, which to do justly must be done with equality, and with a due regard to the nature and circumstances of each individual: a knowledge of these consequently becomes of the first objects of the moralist. But these alone are not sufficient; and it is even necessary to possess information of the degree of happiness or pain which any individual has felt or is likely to feel during its life, before we can determine the justness of its feelings at any particular time, as each individual should have his share, though this knowledge itself is imperfect, as it cannot penetrate into the state of the individual *prior* to, and in the *future* of this life (see Theorem 8, in the sequel). But the constant pursuit of a moralist is to render all beings EQUALLY HAPPY, to increase the stock of happiness, and to lessen the stock of pain, as far as is in his power; these are the keystones on which all the rest depend, on these my own ideas rest, and this is serving God.

CHAPTER IV

Moral reflections, comprising definitions and axioms. What subjects are to be considered in moral questions. Theorem 1. Personal identity, and its connection with a future state; and corollary, showing how an immense increase of animals may be impossible. Relation of time and sensation. On the extent of the will. Theorem 2. On the same subject. Advantage which the general knowledge of this theorem would bestow on society. Theorem 3. Punishment never right, without some other object. Theorem 4. Revenge not always wrong. Theorem 5. When there are a number of different species of animals which destroy each other, the innocent and the guilty are the alternate ones. Question 1. If a guilty being should be punished when the punishment affects an innocent being also? Question 2. When one being would destroy another by accident, if the former should be destroyed or not? Question 3. If a being, A, intends to destroy an innocent being, B, and besides that has the power and the will to perform a great good to a third being, C, whether or not he should be destroyed? Theorem 6. That reason would lead us to suppose if man should exist in a future state, that brutes do also. Theorem 7. That they have no recollection of this life. Question 4. How to distribute good to two unequal beings. Theorem 8. Modification of the latter subject. Petition societies.

———

WE will now lay down some definitions and axioms, and refer to them occasionally; the same appearing also to apply to many other subjects not here treated of, and some of the definitions and axioms not even being made use of. But before we proceed, it will be proper again to notice that they only relate to simple moral ideas, unconnected with any article of faith, leaving the latter subject to the consideration of others, and which should form a subject of itself.

Definition 1. *Positive Actions*

Positive actions we will denominate those actions which require an exertion of the will to perform.

Definition 2. *Negative Actions*

Negative actions are those actions which are merely suffered, without any exertion of the will to prevent them.

Axiom 1. That it is better that the sum of happiness or misery of all animals during their whole existence, be equal than unequal, provided that the quantity of happiness or misery of them all together be the same in the one case as in the other; the same also applying between every two animals, unless injustice should result from it to a third animal or identical self (which will be explained later), or in other words, to a third animal born or unborn.

But this life being the only state that we have any acquaintance with, we must in our actions concerning the happiness of others in this life, be guided by circumstances of this life alone; though in judging further of the ways of Providence, we must view this life as probably being only part of a whole, consisting of other states also.

Axiom 2. That if there should be a certain quantity of good or evil to bestow or inflict on two individuals, which were equal and similar in every respect, it should be equally divided.

Axiom 3. That every animal is better acquainted with its own feelings than it is of the feelings of others, and consequently better acquainted with its own feelings than any other animals can be of them.

Axiom 4. That as far as any animal knows the results of his own actions, he will generally do the best for himself.

Axiom 5. That we should never admit of the propriety of the will or volition of one animal being the agent of another, unless we should perceive its own good to result from it, or that justice should require it.

Axiom 6. That it seems generally better for an animal to

suffer from its own error, than that the error should be the cause of equal sufferings to another: because the suffering, or the expectation of the suffering to result from the error, while the mind is deliberating, may be the means of its cure or of its prevention; and this axiom particularly applies where the error may have given to the performer more good or less evil than his share.

Axiom 7. That positive crimes are worse than negative crimes, and positive virtues better than negative virtues, provided that the extent of them be the same.

Axiom 8. That the importance of any action is measured by the degree of pleasure or pain that it causes or prevents.

Axiom 9. That the greater the quantity of happiness, and the less the quantity of pain in every animal, the better it will be, unless evil to others arise in consequence.

But those subjects which should be continually borne in mind in questions of morality, as far as they respect natural reasoning, are as follows:

Firstly. The nature of personal identity.

Secondly. The nature of time, as it relates to sensation.

Thirdly. The nature and extent of the will of an animal.

For want of a just idea of personal identity, a due regard cannot be possessed of giving a compensation to a being which had suffered pain. Ignorance of the nature of time will deprive us of a measure for the sensations of animals. And a false idea of the nature of volition is one of the evils by which the greatest cruelties become committed.

THEOREM I
PERSONAL IDENTITY, OR IDENTICAL SELF

Personal identity has been studiously considered by the great Mr. Locke, by Vin Perronet, and by other philosophers: but as the term has frequently been used with different ideas attached to it, I will attempt to define that idea which I mean the term to express.

Every animal possesses *something* which distinguishes it

from all other animals; and this is what I understand by *personal identity*, or rather the *identical self*. This in every animal is perfectly distinct and indivisible, since the only knowledge we have of it is when it is entire; and divisibility of this is what we cannot conceive: but if indivisible, it must also be indestructible, and must always have existed. It is not possessed of any kind of consciousness: but no consciousness can, it appears, exist without it; as life itself seems to be composed of *personal identity*, and other essentials of the mind or body, and that it is the *combination* which produces consciousness.

This is the only essential of the mind which never alters in the slightest degree; and every person is just the same self at all times.

All *identical selves* appear to be perfectly similar in their *nature*, yet not in their *circumstances*: as for instance, two pieces of *iron* which though alike in their nature, may be in different places, or in different positions from each other.

That every identical self is capable of producing, or of contributing to produce, any kind of sensation which the mind or body it belongs to, will admit of.

We are partly bound to attribute these two last qualities to *personal identity*, from the fact that we draw our ideas of its nature without regard to the difference of sensations of the person or mind of which it forms a part. But if indestructible, of course it remains after death, though in a state of unconsciousness.

It is further evident, that if it could then be united to another body as before, it would be again brought into animation; and being always in the power, and in the knowledge of God (as it was before this life), it may not be presumption to suppose that this will some time be done. Many persons, however, do not perceive any more probability for it to happen, than for a table to be made animated: but this is absurd; for let us suppose a table to have animation bestowed upon it, then the table must be so modelled as to give sensation to some identical self. But what *identical self* is it to refer to? There is not any one that has more connection with the table than another has; consequently the idea is vague: as by the first argument every identical self existed before. Therefore instead of giving animation to the table, we can only conceive that the table might be so contrived as to give consciousness or sensation to some *identical self*, but not to any which had never existed before, because there are none; and the action will then be changed, from animating the table to animating some *identical self* which has previously existed, and of converting the table into the body of it.

Even if the existence of substance or matter itself be erroneous, according to the ideas of some philosophers, the nature of *personal identity* seems not to be affected by it, and *must* be attached to mind to produce consciousness.

It is also evident that no one man can distinguish the difference between the identity of two other men.

But every man knows his own identity, though he knows no other; and is never in danger of mistaking himself for another person.

It appears that a man, G, has not any more knowledge of the identity of his dearest friend, E, than he has of that of an utter stranger, F, and that all his affections are bestowed upon the mechanism of his friend's body, and the qualities of his mind, which seem entirely to depend on it. The mechanism being joined to an *identical self* which is unknown to G, the *body* of E being the only thing that G has any kind of knowledge of; and if it were possible to place another person, F, before G, instead of his friend E, who perfectly resembled him in looks, in actions, and in recollection of the same past events, and this were done, G would certainly mistake F for his real friend E, and would never discover his error.

That this is not a far fetched thought is manifest by the fact that after a person has been for a long while absent from his own children, he is obliged to ask their names before he knows them. The mother herself might be deceived by placing a strange infant in the cradle of her own, and would cherish it without knowing any difference.

It is difficult to say what the parent means when she asks the name of her child, and what more she knows when she is told; unless it refers to some of the past actions of the child. It is certain, however, that she suspends her affection for it till she is told that it is her own, though the *personal identity* of the child is entirely concealed from her even after she has been told.

Corollary. It likewise appears not absurd to surmise, that the power of production of animals would cease, if their numbers should amount to a certain magnitude; because, there is no apparent necessity for supposing that the number of *identical selves* must be infinite: but if finite, when they were once united to bodies, so as to constitute animals, it would be impossible for any more animals to be born, for want of identical selves; and this number may not be immensely great.

Nature of the relation between TIME *and* SENSATION

We do not intend in this short treatise to enter into the abstruse subject of *time*, any further than just to give the hint that we must not entirely trust to our own measure of time for a knowledge of the duration of the sufferings or enjoyments of another animal, but must add further reflection and observation to correct our estimate on this important subject; as it seems that the same length of time which appears a minute to one animal, may represent a century to another, and must depend entirely on the quickness of their sensations.

Natural observations on the power and extent of the WILL *of a person, or other animal*

The nature of the *will* of a person, or other animal, is a subject which has caused much perplexity, and is in my opinion generally misunderstood; also that far greater powers are ascribed to it than can be proved to be correct. The ideas which I should think must result simply from natural reflections are as follows:

That the *will* of every animal is merely to be considered as a kind of laboratory, where the actions of the animal are willed; that it to say, where the judgement determines to put its desires in execution, and actually commences the operation. But it is evident that it must be governed by something, that it is not a first cause; and the following conclusions, I think, may be deduced from these ideas, which we will call

THEOREM 2. That according to the notions which we should entertain of the nature of the actions of man, and of other animals, from natural reflections, neither of them have ever possessed the power to have omitted any action which they *have* performed, or to have performed any action which they have *not* performed.

Apparent proof. Whatever has been done, was once going to be done; but if prevented, it would not have been going to be done, and would not have been done, which is contrary to the hypothesis. Similar reasoning also applying to the omission of any action.

Yet all the actions of every animal, excepting convulsive motions, become effected by the operations of the will, and cannot be performed against it. But then the will itself is governed by causes which the person or animal cannot control; by the mechanism of his body, by the will of the Almighty, and by fate itself.

I am aware that this opinion meets with much opposition; and it is objected that we should then have no command over our actions, also that we might suffer the greatest injuries to befall us, without attempting to prevent them, because "whatever is to be will be." But this is erroneous: because although we have no command over our *will*, our will has command over our actions; and as observed by Seneca, when we suffer an evil to have its scope, our will is determined not to prevent it; but when we ward it off, our will is determined to ward it off; and, as before remarked, it seems that the mechanism of the body when good, is so contrived as to produce appropriate desires and feelings upon every occasion, and thus determines the will: but when the actions are bad, that it is owing to some fault in the mechanism. Though we are not to infer by this, that men and other animals are bare machines, because they are each possessed of an identical self, and perhaps of other essentials, which a clock is destitute of.

Locke says, in his Essay on Human Understanding, book ii. chapter 21 : 23,2: "That willing, or volition, being an action, and freedom consisting in a power of acting or not acting, *a man in respect of willing, or the act of volition, when any action in his power is once proposed to his thoughts as presently to be done, cannot be free.*"

The opponents to this doctrine likewise say, if we could not have prevented our doing a bad action, we ought not to be punished for it. The answer is, that although we could not have prevented the bad action, the punishment is still necessary, because it operates properly on the mechanism which produced the sensations that determined the will to perform evil, thus preventing a repetition of it; also, by the force of example, to prevent others from committing the same fault.

It may further be questioned, what *right* we have to punish a person for a crime which he could not have prevented himself from committing?

But the reply to this consists of Axiom 6, that it seems generally better for an animal to suffer from his own error, than that the error should be the cause of equal sufferings to another.

The knowledge of this theory is of the utmost importance in most of the concerns of life: for while it allows of a limited and necessary degree of punishment in crimes, it disowns every act which exceeds the bounds of necessity and moderation; it suits the punishment to the crime, and never goes beyond it. It shows the fallacy of the pretended justification of cruelty to criminals, on the plea of its being caused by their own fault; and it commands that the punishment should not exceed the degree of mischief arising from the crime.

But here is presented a difficulty, which consists in determining what degree of punishment is due to an individual who commits a crime that produces an ill effect on several other persons; whether the punishment should be much greater than when the effects are only felt by one?

Without pretending, however, to give a satisfactory answer to this, I am rather of opinion that it is repugnant to good feelings for the punishment very far to exceed the injury; though I conceive that it should in some degree.

THEOREM 3. It likewise seems obvious that punishment can never be right for any crime merely for the sake of the punishment, unconnected with the production of good effect; and that a criminal who should fail in executing any evil design meeting with punishment instead, merits commiseration quite as much as a good person who suffers equally; excepting in cases where the commiseration would prevent the effects of justice from having their full force. For instance, suppose a man having committed a crime should perceive his own error, and from due reflection on it, should become a man of good morals, without his amendment being publicly known. Then, if it were only made to appear to others that this man were punished, it would be sufficient, and he ought not then actually to suffer; or even if he did not become good, but was prevented by his death being near at hand, or by any other cause, from committing crimes again, then also it would be best only for it to appear as though he were punished, without being so in reality. See Axiom 9.

THEOREM 4. But though the preceding theorem teaches that all punishment which is unproductive of good effect is wrong, we are not it seems to infer from thence, that the feeling of revenge is always improper. This is a nice and delicate topic to venture upon: but under whatever garb truth may appear, it is our business to find it out; and I must confess that in some cases the feeling of revenge, when confined to moderation, appears not only excusable, but even laudable. Though I am aware that this passion is generally deprecated by the most virtuous, even Aristotle having incurred the censure of Seneca for defending it, the case appears to me thus:

That the passion of revenge is not generally felt when the judgement is sufficiently strong to perceive that punishment is in itself bad; that is to be understood, when inflicted merely to produce pain, without some advantage arising in consequence. But when the necessity of punishment, in order to prevent evil or to produce good, is apparent, then a desire to punish may exist solely for those purposes. Still, when the sensation from the injury overcomes the understanding, it seems then not unjust that a person should, for his own benefit, give way to a certain latitude of revenge, unless he should be able to feel pleasure in forgiving the injury instead; but which mode, of course, would be wrong to adopt, when forgiving the injury would be injurious: because,

By Axiom 1, all animals should be equal in degrees of happiness; and when one being, A, receives an injury from another being, B (both being equal), the situation of A becomes worse than that of B, by the act of B (see Axiom 6): therefore if A should possess a passion of revenge, in gratifying which he would receive pleasure, and generate pain in B, so as to restore the balance of pleasure and pain, the evil would then become compensated. And in this case it even seems right that his understanding should give some way to his feelings; otherwise he would suffer more evil than his share. It is ridiculous to think it right to do good to a person who has injured us, only from the idea of that being the most *noble* and most *effective* mode of *retaliation*; because if the good done in return acts so as to produce his mortification, it is just as much revenge as any other sort of retaliation would be; and those who applaud their forbearance in such an act, should know that they choose a more severe mode of revenge than he who would retaliate in the plain way. But revenge should not descend to cruelty: it should not cause retaliation with more force than the injury received, and should seldom be given way to at all; because in most cases the benefit the revengeful receive is trifling in proportion to the injury done to the aggressor.

This passion, though generally odious, when it arises in a discreet person, and particularly when it is kindled by great injuries done to a third being, seems to me rather to proceed from virtue than from vice, and sometimes causes us to act right when judgement itself fails. It has generally been alleged, that if we once suffer our reason to give some way, we lose entire command over our actions: but this wants proof; and the extent of our actions must be determined while the reason is strong, and attended to afterwards. It is to be observed, that the misunderstanding and the energies of the mind and body are not always sufficiently strong to act alone in every case, and that they require the assistance of the passions to give them their due force, for which wise purpose they seem to have been intended.

Besides, it is to be noticed, that when punishment becomes necessary, it would be performing a very painful task to inflict it unaccompanied with some temporary feelings of resentment or aversion towards the object; unless the operator should be almost destitute of concern for the sufferings of all others; and by growing accustomed to punish persons without having their benefit in view, not having been previously excited by some sensations of resentment, he would spoil the quality of his own general feelings for others, and become capable of inflicting pain on them without remorse, when on the most friendly terms, the moment he should judge it necessary.

THEOREM 5. If there be two equal beings, A and B, and that it would be in the power and intention of A to destroy B unjustly for his own benefit, but for a third being C, which can by destroying A prevent him from destroying B. It seems right then that C should rather destroy A, because it would prevent the destruction of B unjustly.

Admitting the difficulty of demonstrating this, it does not appear absolutely necessary to do so, because it is a law that is generally acknowledged, and upon which the principles of self-defence and all our ideas of justice depend; and experience telling us, that the only way in which we can exist is to adopt it as a law.

This being granted, suppose a fourth being, D, should attempt to destroy C, to prevent C from destroying A, then it seems that D would be guilty of a similar crime in attempting to destroy C, that A was in attempting the destruction of B: because C having acted justly, should not be destroyed; and D should rather be destroyed, to prevent him from destroying C. We will further suppose that a fifth being, E, comes and attempts to destroy D: then E is by the same argument not guilty. Thus, whatever number of beings act in this manner, their alternate actions become innocent and guilty. The first innocent, the second guilty, the third innocent, the fourth guilty and the fifth innocent and so for the rest.

Question 1. Suppose a being, A, requires punishment, but that he cannot be punished without also punishing another being B: Ought A to be punished notwithstanding?

Observation. A general reply to this question would be attended with great difficulty. But its importance seems to demand the attention of every one, and it seems to me to depend greatly on whether the act of punishing B would be positive or negative: if positive, that is to say if done with the intention of punishing B, then it appears that the punishment of A should rather be abstained from than to punish B also. For example: Suppose an army, A, unjustly attacks another army, B, and at the same time A places in its own front a number of innocent men, so that the army B cannot return the fire of the army A, without shooting the innocent men first. I should rather think in this case that strict justice would prevent B from returning the fire of A: though I am undecided: as perhaps the crime would only fall on A, for having placed the innocent men in the way of B. But if the innocent men had come there by accident, then it seems that B would be committing a *positive action* in firing upon them, and that it would then be decidedly unjust, unless they had agreed to it.

The negative case is, when the punishment to B is not directed to him, and only proceeds from his dependence on A. As for example: Suppose A was going to be executed for a crime, and B being the friend of A should become punished in consequence of his affection for A. The answer of this is also difficult, and though the punishment of A cannot always be abstained from, on account of the punishment that B would receive in consequence, I am of opinion that in many cases the punishment of A should be mitigated on account of B - though I do not pretend to decide either of these cases.

Question 2. If a being, A, would, if not prevented by his own destruction, destroy another being, B, by *accident*, would it then be just or unjust of a third being, C, to destroy A to prevent him from accidentally destroying B?

We will abstain at present from any absolute answer to this, and leave it to the consideration of others. But it seems wrong that A should commit any act which should even unintentionally deprive B of his *right*, and that A should rather be destroyed himself.

Question 3. If a being, A, would destroy an innocent being, B, intentionally, and besides that, would have the power and the will, if he should live, to perform a great good to a third being C. Should A be destroyed or not, no other preventive appearing possible?

I will not at present attempt to answer this; but will only observe, that it does not seem that we have any right to preserve a being A, that would cause the destruction of another being, B, on account of good which he should cause to a third being C; because this would be depriving B of his good, and giving it to C.

THEOREM 6. That Reason would lead us to suppose, if Man should exist in a future state, that brutes do also.

Because by Theorem 1, as the personal identity of all animals seems to be similar, and as this appears to be the only part of an animal which remains after death, we have the same reason to suppose that one of them may experience a future state of animation as another, nothing remaining whereby we can give a preference to either of them, as to the probability.

THEOREM 7. That reason would also lead us to surmise, that if a future state of animation should be the lot of man and other animals, they will then not have any recollection of this life.

Because, if the personal identity be the only thing that remains, and which memory does not refer to, there will be nothing for the recollection to be attached to.

It may also be reasonable to expect, that if there be a future state, those persons or animals who have had most suffering in this life, or in a prior state, will generally have a greater share of enjoyment in the future state, and even *vice versa*; which idea accords with our notion of the justness of God. But it is not to be inferred from thence that any injury which we may cause to another, will not be real harm, on account of the injured being afterwards meeting with compensation: because, even if we should be able to render the whole sum of good and evil of one being equal to that of another, the actions of every person might tend to increase the general stock of good and evil, according to their justness; and because it may not in all cases be possible for the share of happiness of one to be rendered equal to that of another.

Question 4. Suppose A and B were both suffering equally for want of some particular thing, as food, and there should be a quantity of food to be distributed among them which should not be equal to their wants. But suppose A and B, each of whom required an equal quantity to be satisfied with, were in other respects of pleasure and pain *unequal.* Ought their share of the food to be in proportion to their want of food alone, or to their want of food combined with their other circumstances of happiness and misery?

It appears to me that their quantity of food should not be equal; but that if A suffer more misery in one respect, he should enjoy more happiness in another; and that the quantity of food should be guided by their want of it, combined with their other degrees of happiness and misery, which it seems would render them more equal; the sum of pleasure and pain of the two being fixed, and one being unable to have a greater share without causing the other to have less. (See Axiom 1).

THEOREM 8. That if we have the power of bestowing some good upon two beings, the one having enjoyed less good during its existence than the other, we ought, it appears, in preference to bestow it on that one which had previously enjoyed the least, other circumstances being equal or similar.

By Axiom 1 this appears to be the case. It however seems difficult to assign a reason why past sufferings should be taken into account, the nature of the identical self not being altered by them; because, if the sufferings be past, how can they affect the present? The answer is, that although they do not affect the present, they affect the whole: and should we not admit the justness of this theorem, we must also dispute the justice of our saving any good to enjoy at a future period, because, if others should not do the same, we should then be enjoying more than our share. But it is obvious that it is of no importance to others whether we choose to enjoy our own good at the present, or at the future time; therefore let us admit of the justice of exchanging the time, and then this theorem will also appear just.

It is besides apparent, that the exchanging of the time of enjoying any good is not generally considered of much importance, and that we should frequently think little of postponing an enjoyment, when we should grieve to yield it up. The practice of this theorem, however, is attended with great difficulty, particularly as no exact parallel can be drawn between different kinds of goods or evils.

PETITION SOCIETIES

But before we quit our observations on morality, it remains again to express our regret that moral inquiries seem lately to have given way to other subjects: so much so indeed, that scarcely a question can be put, but it is immediately silenced by some reply drawn from other sources than those of bare morality or true religion; and instead of gaining knowledge by the force of reason, we fall into error by the weakness of prejudice. To remedy this grievance I would recommend a plan, which, though it cannot boast of much novelty, might nevertheless be productive of happy results: and it would consist in the establishment of *societies*, where the business should be to investigate and to discuss all moral subjects and customs, to form reports of the same, and to present *petitions* to Parliament on any improvements suggested.

These societies should comprise different classes of persons of both sexes, and of all ranks; but only those of good characters and abilities admitted, and the chief should consist of such as were of studious and retired habits, and who devoted much time to the study of morality; also of persons who have had most intercourse with mankind; some members of Parliament should join them, and they might be termed Petition Societies.

CHAPTER V

Argument between Y and Z. The right or injustice of slaughtering animals for food contested; and of those which are suspected of being dangerous and obnoxious. Of using animal food which has been slaughtered. Remarks on the animalcula in water. Further remarks on slaughtering animals.

———

Y: I UNDERSTAND that you act in opposition to the laws of God, of nature, and of man; that you deny the very first elements of those laws by which the world is governed; that through a pretended or mistaken aim at perfection, and in attempting to compass things far beyond your reach, you misapply your exertions and fail in your grasp; you set your face against the precepts of your forefathers, and of the most learned of all ages in every civilized country in the world, and set up your own judgement in opposition to them all. Scarcely with the support of a single partisan to share in your presumptuous innovations on the established principles of society, do you attack, and wish to overturn them, without having any thing to offer in lieu, but vain chimeras, the produce of vitiated feelings, and a diseased brain. Thus, while you attempt to create new theories, you only breed confusion, and lose yourself in the labyrinth where you have undertaken to lead others.

Z: These are serious accusations! But though I confess that my laws differ in many points from those of the generality of mankind, I trust that they are not of opposition to the purpose of God. If you blame me for not paying blind obedience to the established customs of man, I own to the charge; but how much more culpable should I be, were I to adopt those tenets which are in contrariety to my own conscience! God has furnished every man with reason, and God *demands* him to exert it in the regulation of his conduct. If then he commit an error while following the guidance of others, the fault is still is own; and consists in not using that judgment by which his own actions should first be weighed. Besides, even in pursuing the dictates of others, his judgment must first give the assent to one of the various opinions of others whereby he is to be led; and thus in spite of himself his reason will have its way, whether he consults it or not. If I endeavour to compass more than I am able, I may find where I am stopped; if I attempt less, I remain ignorant of my strength. I confess I cannot always see clearly: but it seems that though you act differently, your sight is as treacherous as mine. However, where are your charges? I will yield to demonstration, but not to assertion.

Y: In the first place, you dispute the right invested in mankind of slaughtering other animals for food, and of compelling them to labour for his benefit, for which purpose they have been created, their flesh and their services have been made palatable and necessary to man, without the nourishment of which he would soon grow sickly and unfit for his station - his life would be painful - his death premature.

Z: First, how do you prove that mankind is invested with the right of killing them, and that brutes have been created for the purpose you assert them to be? Secondly, it is to be observed that the flesh of man himself possesses the same nourishing and palatable qualities? And are we then to become cannibals for that reason? I grant that the health of man requires animal food, and it is not to be expected that the strength and faculties of either the body or the mind can be near as great with the privation of it, as with its aid; but that is nothing to the animals; a robber would not be so rich if he were not to steal; it is not therefore right to steal, when the laws can be evaded.

Y: It is evident that the right has been invested in man; first, because he has been furnished with the power, and because his life is of the most importance. Secondly, it is better for the animals themselves: they would otherwise grow so numerous as not only to destroy each other; there would be nothing to be seen but animals starving and dying of all manner of diseases, without receiving any succour or attention from their own kind. Is it not better that we should cause them to have a short and happy life, than a long and miserable one?

Z: Then it is right for one man to kill another, if he fear not the laws of his country, and if he fancy that it is to the benefit of the other. It is besides not quite proved to me that his life is more important (see observations on the subject in this work in answer to it). But even allowing it to be so, the two are unconnected with each other, and I do not see what right one animal has to deprive another of its small importance, to prevent himself from losing more: if this theory be generally admitted, a young man might kill an old man, to save his own longer expectant life. And are we authorized to kill one animal for the benefit of another of its species? If they should overstock the world, it will then be time to begin to destroy them. It seems however more just that nature should take her course, and that man should be neutral till provoked. It is certainly easier for him to destroy others than to suffer inconvenience himself; but that does not make it right. We have not however at present any reason to complain of the too great fecundity of those animals we use for food, etc., and we even take great pains to produce them, not for their own enjoyment, but for the good and pleasure we derive by destroying and tormenting them.

Y: However that may be, man must not kill his own kind; it is contrary to the law of nature. Besides, how soon would even a single cod-fish, which it is said produces 9,000,000 of eggs, overstock the ocean!

Z: First, I deny the fact that it would be contrary to the laws of nature; pikes, rats and tigers even devour their own kind: and how are you informed that they would overstock the ocean, or that their fecundity may not bear some kind of proportion to their destruction, and that their power of increasing may not be limited? (See Corollary to Theorem 1).

Y: Because we cannot suppose that the fecundity of one being can be at all influenced by the destruction of another, from which it is totally distinct.

Z: Recollect, that though distinct, they are each a part of one system, and of which system we are ignorant: for aught we know, only a certain number of beings may be capable of existence (see the article on Identity), and that these become born when there are vacancies, or opportunities.

Y: Then if this be so, we create when we destroy, and we give a little existence to many, instead of a long life to one.

Z: No, they might all have their share in time (see article on Identity); and the shorter their lives were, the oftener would they undergo the pains of birth and death.

Y: We are talking of things beyond our reach.

Z: You began the subject, by asserting that the world would be overstocked.

Y: It is before my eyes.

Z: It is not before mine.

Y: We have instances of some species of animals which have at one time been numerous, and, owing to their obnoxious qualities, have been destroyed in great numbers, for instance the wolves in England. Why then are not wolves possessed of such a fecundity as always to keep up the same number?

Z: I do not consider it impossible for any species of animals to be reduced or even destroyed. Still it may be impossible for it to exceed a certain limit: therefore, though we may justly or unjustly remedy the evil of a limited overstock, by destroying them; we may not be in danger of an increase beyond a certain extent. You have given me an example of many wolves having once existed, and of a great reduction having taken place; but you cannot produce an instance where an immoderate and injurious increase of any animal has obtained, without a reduction having soon followed. Besides there is reason to think that other animals have become more numerous in consequence of the decrease of wolves; and that when the fecundity of one animal become inadequate to the task, that of other animals may supply the deficiency.

Y: Suppose the fecundity should exceed the destruction, how dreadful would be the consequence! Famine would exist in the midst of plenty, and the destruction of one animal by another would continually prevail.

Z: Why so? If they were to destroy one another, we should get rid of them: and if they were to starve, the bodies of some animals would also be food for the rest.

Y: Might man not as well kill an ox, as that it should be killed by a tiger?

Z: No; his death could not be known beforehand, much less could the time and manner of its taking place be ascertained.

Y: Even admitting that increase shall be in proportion to destruction throughout the universe, you cannot suppose that this principle would obtain partially: for instance, if you had a cat and you were not to destroy its kittens, would not your own dwelling and your property soon be over-run by them? And would it not be better to kill them when first born, than to suffer them to starve when mature, or to starve yourself in the attempt to save them?

Z: I do not pretend that the principle would obtain partially, and I am aware of the difficulty of partially acting upon it. I have also to observe, that the intention of a person in destroying them entirely for their own benefit, may be a virtuous one; but perhaps an undue authority, as a great partial overflow would in fact be a small general overflow, and the animals composing it would be entitled to a share of the provisions afforded by nature, but not particularly to the property of the person under whose roof they had been produced; and if they should be allowed to starve, the fault would also fall on other persons.

Y: You would save birds and mice by destroying the kittens?

Z: And cause the destruction of insects and worms.

Y: Then why not destroy the birds and mice yourself?

Z: As the case is difficult, I should prefer to be neutral till I shall possess more knowledge (see Theorem 5), and as we should never suppose an animal guilty till found in an act of guilt. It is to be recollected, that men themselves are guilty of the same crime of slaughter as the cats are, and that similar reasoning applies to each.

Y: Cats multiply prodigiously, while human beings seldom do more than continue their race; therefore the life of the individuals of the latter must be of the most importance.

Z: This distinction does not only relate to man; as the smaller the animal, and the shorter its life, the greater is generally the increase: besides, there are countries where men even destroy their own children; you do not approve of this, I presume?

Y: No.

Z: And what are your opinions concerning the necessity of war? As this is also one of the means of diminishing population, you would not, I should conclude, encourage it for that purpose?

Y: I would not.

Z: But you would encourage the destruction of other animals as a means of preventing evil, and not that of mankind; are you certain you are not partial?

Y: I must confess that the subject relating to man seems

more serious, as I conceive him to be superior. What do you think of the propriety of killing a dangerous animal in self-defence - should that be done?

Z: When it has shown a disposition to attack, but not before.

Y: Then are we to wait till we are half-killed before we defend ourselves?

Z: No; mankind possesses sufficient ingenuity, when assisted by prudence and diligence, to discover this propensity without incurring much danger; and it is not just to become the assailant, only because we fear being attacked, without the disposition of attacking having been discovered.

Y;   Will you not allow there to be a difference between the consequences of killing a human being and a brute? In the latter case the act stops there: but in the former you render the relatives unhappy; and secondly, by preventing security in society, you would destroy society altogether.

Z: Would that I could discover the affection of man for his relatives, to surpass that of brutes! (See remarks on this subject here). And it is manifest that animals which are used for food seem to be aware of their danger, also, they fly from man, and some of them, for instance the hare and its kind, have evidently from habit the tokens of continual fear depicted in their appearance. Who is ignorant that a sheep dreads a butcher's shop? And that in China, where dogs are eaten, the dogs know their butchers, and will fly on them. These are facts, however unaccountable they may be. Whether they have power in any way to communicate their feelings to each other, is not for us to determine. It is true that a well domesticated animal will not possess this fear, but will love his master, is he to be killed for that?

Y: I understand that you conceive animals generally to be ill-treated and unhappy, if so, do we not yield them a service in killing them?

Z: They are mostly unhappy because we render them so,

and if they are not to be killed, of course they are not to be ill-treated.

Y: But this does not depend on one man: if *he* should not ill-treat them, *others* would.

Z: I grant that it appears you would generally save them much misery by it; but what right have we to dispose of their fates? And though I conceive most animals (including man in all states of life) generally to be in a state of suffering, I have sufficient veneration for God, not to suppose that it will be for the best in the end; and that as they *are* created, they should *remain* so; otherwise we should have nothing to do when we saw any person afflicted with a lasting malady but to kill him.

Y: Do you then really assert it to be a crime for man to kill other animals for food?

Z: I do not assert it, but I conceive it to be.

Y: Do you conceive it to be if his life depend on it - and that it would be wrong for a man on the point of starving to kill an animal for his support?

Z: I am inclined to think that it would.

Y: Would you conceive it to be wrong also for him to eat the flesh of an animal after it had been killed by a butcher, without his order, and against his wish?

Z: Though this may not be absolute crime, it may be an act which had better be avoided. In the former case, I conceive that a person would be committing crime, but in the latter, only unintentionally encouraging a repetition of crime in others; the degree of *wrong* in this action will partly depend on the motive of the performer, which will be hereafter explained.

Y: Do you include those animals which are guilty of the same crime themselves by living on prey? Should we not then save a thousand lives by killing one?

Z: We must never suppose a person or an animal guilty until they are found in the act, and then we must investigate the nature of the crime. It is true that the animal living by slaughter may be less entitled to our consideration than the animal which is harmless; but recollect, the former may plead the same excuse itself, unless his slaughter be only of those animals which live on vegetables; and then, though justice may require their destruction, it would be repugnant to the feelings of humanity to slaughter them with that plea, unless we could quite assure our conscience that our design in killing them was more to prevent their doing mischief than for our own benefit: besides, we might then extend this principle still further, and kill our own species because they are also animals of prey. It is moreover to be observed, that if one carnivorous animal kills another, he may save lives by it also, and the nature of the act will be different according to circumstances. (See Theorem 5). And, further, it will frequently be impossible to discover when the animal becomes guilty or innocent, as it depends on such a variety of circumstances: we should therefore be more safe from infringing the laws of moral rectitude, not to interfere in this case.

Y: Then I conclude, that though you do not consider this so wrong, you incline to think it not right, and that at least it is repugnant to your feelings?

Z: This is exactly the case.

Y: I suppose you also deem it a crime to *drink*, as you destroy myriads of animals in the water of every draught?

Z: I consider this an evil, but not a crime, because I do not cause or wish them to be there, and would assist them to escape if possible. They have no more claim to the water than I have; and we know so little of the nature of these animals, that we are not even sure that they die when the water is drunk; the very fact of their being there is concealed from us, and but for the microscope we should never have known it. I however consider it wrong to waste water in any way which may injure the animalcula.

Y: You say that if one animal should kill another which is innocent, for food, you would not consider it the same crime to kill the former as if it were not charged with that act; then do not the most harmless animals kill not only animalcula in their drink, but insects on their grass?

Z: This is undesignedly done.

Y: Then I suppose you call the one murder, and the other an act resembling justifiable homicide? Do you imagine that a cow is able to distinguish the difference between the morality of the two actions, and that it should be punished in the same way that a rational being should be?

Z: Whether or not a cow knows the difference, the crime is much the same. I do not conceive that either a man or a brute deserves punishment for crimes any further than what is necessary for the benefit of others, or the improvement of itself; and as unexplained punishment to a brute is not so likely to act as an example to others, or as a lesson to itself, it is of course less necessary to inflict it; but still the same laws of justice apply where it can prevent the evil.

Y: What does an insect care, when it is killed, whether the animal which kills it acts up to one doctrine or another? And why not prevent it by putting the animal to death in one case as well as in the other?

Z: What does a man care whether he is killed by another committing murder or by accident? Still the punishment of the latter is, and is justly, very different to the former.

Y: But if the assassin prove to be insane, whereby he becomes more on a level with a brute, he is justly pardoned, though the person cared not in being killed whether the other was sane or not: this proves that a being devoid of reason is, and is justly, not even considered to be capable of committing crime: therefore your distinction between an animal which kills another designedly or undesignedly falls to nought.

Z: Then neither ought to be killed.

Y: No, not if the evil can be prevented without; but if not, they would both equally deserve death.

Z: Then you make no difference between an animal possessed of reason and one which is not.

Y: Not any further than that the punishment of death to an animal possessed of reason, operates as a preventive to others of its species; but not so to the one devoid of reason, because although a being may guard against committing an act if he be caused to fear the consequence, one devoid of reason cannot have this fear instilled into his mind.

Z: I agree with that; and whether a distinction should be made, or not, appears doubtful. But recollect, by instinct itself we feel an abhorrence to wilful oppression, and by the general law of nature we act against it: not so of accidental injury. Recollect also that a being who commits wilful wrong, at other times commits unintentional mischief also, and is thus the perpetrator of two evils instead of one.

Y: That is certainly true; but suppose the unintentional perpetrator happens to be a larger and more powerful animal, so as to produce much more mischief than the latter, who commits intentional mischief besides, how does the case stand then?

Z: Still I think the intentional one should rather be destroyed than the unintentional one, because he is a worse piece of mechanism, and therefore more prone to commit other faults than the former; but I am not decided on this point. However, I do not allow that the case can precisely appear in nature, because we are far from being certain whether animals have or have not the power of communicating many of their ideas to each other; and whether they cannot in some manner profit by example, as human beings would do.

Y: As you think it wrong for man to kill other animals for food, do you also think it wrong that animals should devour each other? As this is the general law of nature.

Z: It appears wrong, according to the rules by which we

govern our own actions to each other; and should I witness the attempt in any animal of destroying another, I would endeavour to frustrate it; though this might probably be wrong.

Y: Then, if you deem the destruction of one animal by another to be a fault, you blame the Almighty; as he is the author of it.

Z: Such reasoning would teach that there is no fault in any thing, God being the author of it all. And though an evil may exist, its non-existence may have been unavoidable and contradictory; therefore neither the power nor the goodness of God can be questioned for that, as God does nothing which is contradictory.

Y: Then it is not contradictory for animals to destroy each other, because God *is* the cause, and therefore it must be right.

Z: Why should you particularly press this question, with a difficulty that applies equally well to every question which can be proposed? You might as well assert it to be wrong to prevent murder, because when it does happen, God permits it. But you must recollect, that whenever you prevent any bad actions, God allows you to do so; and that your business is to act to the best of your judgment.

Y: Suppose you were to kill one animal in defending another, or in defending yourself from its attack; might you then use it for food?

Z: There could not be any injustice in that, provided the defence was the motive by which you had been actuated.

Y: Tell me how carnivorous animals could live without destroying other animals?

Z: Tell me how the animals they prey on can live, if they be killed?

Y: But the whole *species* of the carnivorous kind would then become extinct. Were they created to be annihilated?

Z: I do not see why the whole species of one animal is

more important than an equal number of another, although that number might not comprise the whole species of the latter: and, besides, it is not proved that the whole species would perish; as some might feed on the bodies of those animals which they might find that were in a fit state; and also upon vegetables, which they will eat occasionally. It is known that wolves will live in the two ways mentioned, when deprived of other means.

Y: Why were their appetites made conformable to animal food?

Z: Seemingly that they may use it when they can obtain it without slaughter.

Y: What were the powers of slaughtering bestowed on them for?

Z: Fancy yourself in their power, and then perhaps you would answer this query yourself; which does not only apply to this case, but to every instance where one person is placed within the reach of the cruelty of another. But in reply to your question; the power of slaughtering may necessarily arise out of those powers that were intended for other purposes; as teeth, claws, strength, and courage, apply to the purposes of eating, climbing, running and self-defence.

Y: Why cannot all animals defend themselves?

Z: I do not pretend to solve this. Still, I do not perceive that it is right for them to be the prey of others, only because unprovided with the means of preventing it. If it should be necessary to admit this, there would be an end at once to all moral inquiry.

Y: To what purpose do you imagine the web of a spider was ordained but to catch insects with? Here the intention of God is evidently manifest. Can we suppose that this beautiful invention was made without an object, when we observe how admirably it accomplishes one of such importance?

Z: However difficult it may be to answer this, it seems as much so, to say why a fly should be endowed with life, if not intended to live.

Y: Why may not a fly be killed by a spider as well as by a disease?

Z: Why may not a spider as well die of a disease of hunger, as a fly of a disease of slaughter, if the former is unable to obtain food without committing slaughter? Besides, I have seen vegetable substances in their webs; though whether they used them for food, or not, I will not pretend to say. But I have further to add, that it may not be wrong for a spider to destroy some kinds of insects, such as are described in Theorem 5, though it may not have the sense to know the difference.

CHAPTER VI

On the use of milk and eggs.

———

Y: I UNDERSTAND that you object to the use of milk; what harm can there be in that?

Z: It was evidently provided for the calf, and not for man.

Y: When the calf is taken away from its mother, it is then a kindness to relieve her of her milk.

Z: But the calf should *not* be taken away.

Y: A cow produces more milk than a calf wants, and it can soon be substituted altogether by other food.

Z: Most probably it is not good for the cow to yield more than what is sufficient for the calf, the flow of which is encouraged when it is taken away from her. And I do not conceive that any other food can be so good for the calf as its mother's milk.

Y: But when a cow has been robbed of her calf, must not her milk be taken from her?

Z: If so, less should be taken every day, till she loses her milk entirely.

Y: What is to be done with that?

Z: The person who had taken the calf from its mother, should not be encouraged to sell the milk. But if the calf should have died by accident, or by disease, there would then be no harm in using as much of the milk as the cow might require to have taken from her; but not more.

Y: What harm does it cause to the cow to keep her milk longer?

Z: It is, most likely, an exhaustion of her constitution.

Y: What harm results to wet nurses, from suckling a second child? *They* do not object to it.

Z: It most likely does them some harm, notwithstanding, as it is an unnatural extension of the operations of the animal economy.

Y: What is your reason for objecting to use eggs?

Z: This is not only a robbery to the hen, but it deprives the chickens (which otherwise would be born) of coming into existence.

Y: But what harm does such a robbery produce? A hen lays more eggs than she can hatch, and as many chickens would come into existence if some of the eggs were taken away, as would if not.

Z: The hen would sooner begin to sit if undisturbed, and not exhaust herself by laying so many eggs; and, when she lays more than she can cover, she can eat them herself. Besides, what right have we to prevent one animal from coming into existence because another will supply its place?

Y: Recollect, then, that a great many lives of smaller animals will be saved by preventing the eggs from being hatched; and this can be done without inflicting pain.

Z: Still we may not be right in preventing life. I do not conceive that we should ever attach a charge to an animal till it has actually committed the act, or till it is preparing for it. Besides, respecting their criminality, or justice, it depends on different circumstances (see Theorem 5).

Y: If you abstain from using any kind of animal food yourself, you cannot consistently procure it to entertain your friends with; and you must, therefore, either treat them with your own fare, or not solicit their society. You would not then offer them similar hospitality to that which others can show their friends.

Z: That is granted. But my sentiments towards them are not the less kind on that account; and the evil will be felt by myself as well as by them, in being deprived of their society in consequence. I should not, however, attempt to prevent my family from entertaining their friends as they thought proper.

CHAPTER VII

On the use of leather, and other animal substances. On using the flesh of animals as food which have *not* been slaughtered. On using stags' horn, and tallow. On the insects etc., which are destroyed by the culture of the ground. On the use of silk, and of sheep's wool.

———

Y: As YOU are determined in these instances not to do any thing that can destroy life, of course you also object to the use of leather, glue, tallow, and many other animal substances: otherwise I must lay the tax of inconsistency to your charge, as an animal can no more live without his skin, etc., than without his flesh.

Z: I agree that the use of these substances is all attended with unpleasant reflections; but I do not prohibit them. Neither will I own to the charge of inconsistency; and, on the contrary, I will maintain, that though the object to the master of possessing the skin of an animal, may sometimes act as an additional temptation to him to kill it, it is generally more to the interest of the master to preserve it on account of its skin.

Y: I do not understand this.

Z: Would not all animals die? And would not all of them yield their skins at their death? Then, by suffering them to live, would not their numbers be increased, and thus yield a greater supply of skins?

Y: That is true; but do you suppose that a farmer could afford to maintain an animal for a number of years only to have his skin when he dies? And for the farmer to cede the use of the flesh for nothing?

Z: Better than he could if the animal did not yield a skin.

And, as to the motive of destroying the animal for his flesh, we are not now discussing that point.

Y: But the question is, whether the skin does not, by increasing the value of the animal when killed, operate so as to increase the motive of slaughtering it?

Z: Not reasonably so; because though it adds to the value of the slaughtered animals, it adds more to the preserved ones, as more skins would result from them.

Y: However this may be, knowledge of mankind shows us that persons would generally rather enjoy a small present good, than wait patiently for a greater; and when the uncertainty of life is considered, this will not appear very unreasonable.

Z: I admit that to be frequently the case, but not that it is general; otherwise persons having property would not purchase annuities, but would spend it direct.

Y: Then do you assert that the value of the skin never does cause or tend to produce the slaughter of the beast?

Z: No, I doubt not; but regret that it frequently must do so. Yet, though the animal is killed partly for his skin, a supply of leather does not depend on its being killed, and is even diminished by it.

Y: Even admitting that what you assert would generally be the case, if the value of the skin should only in a few instances produce the slaughter of the beast, and save a great many others, would you have a right to cause the destruction of the few, to save the many?

Z: No; not by an act of design on any particular beast. But recollect, that if this be a crime, it rests with the perpetrator; and that though I might purchase the skin, I would rather purchase the skin of one which had died a natural death, were it known to me.

Y: Still, it is possible for it to be the cause of its death.

Z: I do not pretend to perfection any more than others.

Y: Besides, the skin of an animal having died of a natural disease, would not be so good.

Z: It would be good enough for me; and the more abundant supply which would then exist, would, I conceive, even do more than make amends to the mass of the public for the quality being rather inferior.

Y: Allowing all you advance to be just, would not the same arguments apply to eating the flesh of animals as of wearing their skins?

Z: No; because a universal disgust prevails at the idea of eating the flesh of an animal which had died of disease; the very laws of our country prohibit it from being sold: therefore, the purchase of the meat necessarily incurs the act of slaughtering the animal.

Y: Pray, would you object yourself, to eat the flesh of an animal that had died of any natural disease, of age, or by accident?

Z: I would not; provided the animal had not died of any complaint which had rendered it unwholesome or offensive. And I further conceive, that after it had undergone the cautious examination of experienced persons, and also the action of the fire in cooking, some of it might be used without incurring much risk; though I cannot speak from experience.

Y: The very idea causes me to shudder.

Z: Then at least recollect, that many animals which have been killed have at the time had diseases also, notwithstanding they did not actually die of them; and that a cut throat itself, though not a natural disease, is still a disease. There are many diseases not more disgusting in their effects, than a cut throat, or a split skull.

Y: I suppose then, you would encourage the sale of this?

Z: Yes.

Y: Then, by the argument that you used concerning the skins, you might encourage the sale of all meat; because, as you say the demand for leather increases the motive for preserving the animal, the demand for meat must do the same.

Z: The case is different, on account of the general disgust which acts as a preventive to the using of the flesh for food, and not to the skin for clothing.

Y: But you give me to understand that this disgust would not affect you thus; and that you would use the meat of the one which had died naturally, but not of the slaughtered one; therefore, in purchasing meat, *you are not accessory to the slaughter*, because *to you* the slaughter is *not a necessary* step to procure and to eat meat, as there would be more meat (according to your theory) were they not slaughtered.

Z: This is a good observation, and the circumstance of a person's preferring to use the slaughtered meat would render the act of purchasing the slaughtered meat much less incorrect; particularly if he had actually lived some length of time on the unslaughtered meat; by which he was become assured that, though he should afterwards purchase the slaughtered meat, he would be more willing to purchase the unslaughtered, and which the butcher robs him of.

Y: This is certainly consistent with what you have advanced, though I should have drawn a contrary conclusion, and should rather object to use the slaughtered, if I had experienced that I could substitute the unslaughtered; as I should then judge that the animal had been killed unnecessarily.

Z: Of course the less the necessity, the greater the crime. But when we had proved to ourselves that we could substitute the unslaughtered for the slaughtered, the act of purchasing the meat would become unconnected with the act of killing the beast, as we would purchase it were it not killed.

Y: Not the same meat.

Z: No, not the same meat; but the slaughtered animal could not be injured, nor the slaughter of other animals sanctioned, nor even encouraged by it, provided we were equally willing to purchase the unslaughtered; and in this case I should consider that the butcher had, by his own act, and by the improper authority of others, or of the laws of his country, robbed us of the unslaughtered meat, and placed the slaughtered in its stead.

Y: And would you encourage him to do this?

Z: No; I would buy of him were he to preserve them; he would then have more to sell, and would make more profit.

Y: Does not the butcher know his own interest best?

Z: The fault lies in those who would only purchase the slaughtered meat.

Y: Then, I conclude you to be of opinion, that when you have once proved to yourself that you would prefer the unslaughtered meat, it would not afterwards be wrong for you to use that which had been slaughtered, contrary to your wish, when you should be unable to procure the former (having been deprived of it by the butcher), because your conscience could not be taxed with the act of the butcher, which had been unjustly sanctioned by the prejudices of other persons, or by improper laws; being sure that you do not give way to those prejudices yourself.

Z: This is well observed; and it would do away with the greatest part of the crime. Yet, though a person might prefer the unslaughtered, he might refuse the slaughtered, as a means of preventing the act; and he could not be quite sure that he would prefer the unslaughtered, as it would be necessary for him to be affected by several circumstances of life, to experience changes of constitution and climate, difference of age, etc., before he could be certain that the diet of the unslaughtered meat would always be acceptable to him; and besides, attending to absolute right and wrong, it is the duty of every man to give a good example; and therefore, should he even be individually right in doing the thing, his preference to the unslaughtered meat would not be sufficiently apparent; and his using the slaughtered meat as others do, would be adding his sanction to the thing he disapproves of.

Y: Then the latter observation also applies to this using of the skin?

Z: So it does in some degree; but the fact also remains, that his increasing the *demand* for skins, increases the necessity of their *not* being killed (for the reasons before given). But this does not apply in the same way to the meat, because the difference between the quality of the skins, may be more than compensated by the much greater number of skins that would result from preserving the beasts; whereas, with regard to the meat, the case is different, as a moderate quantity of good meat would certainly be preferred to a great quantity of bad; and there would be much more difference in the quality of the meat than in that of the skin.

Y: This is a nice distinction! You seem hard pressed.

Z: If it *be* a nice distinction, it as least shows a real difference. All theories and laws are bounded by delicate lines and nice distinctions; and besides this, you must not expect for perfection to be attained by one individual, when the multitude throw obstacles in his way. You might press the subject still further, and say that my theory prevents those who adopt it from using a house, furniture, clothing, etc.; because they generally contain some kind of animal substance, which other persons have procured by improper means. This is straining the point; and if one person sacrifices as much as the conduct of others will permit, he has good reason to conclude that were they to act in concord with him, his own conduct would be more correct, with less sacrifice; and quite certain that he has made one step: though I do not mean this to apply to absolute crime.

Y: I have still to observe, that the skins of many animals, such as seals, beavers, and many others, could not be well obtained without killing these animals.

Z: The skins of these, I should be still more averse to use for clothing, than their flesh for food, the necessity being less.

Y: What do you say that the diet of mankind should consist of?

Z: Of vegetables, and of unslaughtered animal substances (from animals having died a natural death).

Y: Do you not think that the supply of such meat would be very uncertain and variable?

Z: It would to private farmers, and in small villages, but not in great towns; as the laws of chance would ensure a regular supply, and every animal would come in turn.

Y: Would you not have some repugnance to use an animal for food, after its death, which you had taken care of while living, and had become attached to?

Z: I certainly should; but would not hesitate to send it to a market that should be instituted for the purpose.

Y: What is to be done in small villages, when the supply fails, and cannot be procured?

Z: Then vegetables alone must suffice. But there are now means known of preserving meat fresh for a length of time.

Y: You acknowledge that vegetables fall far short of giving the same degree of health and strength, of body or mind, as animal food; then, how are mankind to be adequate to their tasks of mental and bodily labour, when they cannot procure the animal food?

Z: They must work rather less; and if that will not do, it will be their misfortune.

Y: Then you would suffer human beings to fall rather than brutes; at least, such brutes as you call innocent.

Z: Say rather, than positively to cause their death. (See Definitions 1 and 2, and Axiom 7).

Y: I have further to ask, what is to be done, when not only a supply of unslaughtered meat should fail, but also of vegetables? Would you allow yourself to starve, rather than to kill even a graminivorous animal?

Z: I cannot tell beforehand what I would do; it would depend on my fortitude. I think, however, that starving would be the strictest justice of the two.

Y: Then, if you have never been put to this test, others

have. How often do all of a ship's company owe their lives to their nets and to their fowling pieces! And sorry should I be for such valuable men to perish for such scruples. Could you bear to be implicated in being accessory to their starvation, by broaching your doctrines?

Z: It is still, I think, my painful duty to broach those doctrines.

Y: You do not, I should conclude, perceive any impropriety in using stags' horn, as stags shed their horns.

Z: No; but I do not conceive that they yield so much nutriment as good vegetable food does, although they may contain a considerable portion of one of the chief ingredients of meat, namely, gelatine, or jelly. In cases of sickness, however, they seem serviceable.

Y: Could any substitutes be found for whale-oil, tallow, and soap? Animals having died of disease, or age, would not contain much fat.

Z: These substances could be substituted by seed-oils, by oil of cocoa-nuts, which is sold at a cheap rate; by a vegetable tallow, from the tallow-tree; by coal gas; by pitch, etc. Besides which, it is known that a fatty substance is produced by keeping lean flesh immersed, in a box with several holes in it, in a stream; and by other processes. This substance is called adipocire; it combines with alkalies, and forms soap. Some real fat would also exist in every animal, and particularly in those that were killed by accidents.

Y: What do you say about the number of insects and worms you destroy in procuring your vegetables?

Z: That I am sorry for it; but that it is undesignedly done.

Y: That will be but a poor compensation to them for the loss of their lives. (See question 2).

Z: It cannot be helped; it is their misfortune to be in my way: and perhaps it *is* wrong, but a crime of a different nature. The answer, however, to Question 2, is undecided; but refers to the words "deprive B of his *right;*" and on the signification of the word *right* it depends.

Y: Would you reason thus, if human beings were in your way, and if they were immoveably fixed in your wheat field, would you cut your wheat and the men both together?

Z: If my life depended on it, and if I were certain I had more right to the wheat field than they had, then I might perhaps be justified in so doing. But I might relinquish my right if I should choose so to do.

Y: How do you know that you have more right to the vegetables than the insects have?

Z: Because I planted them.

Y: By what authority do you possess the ground?

Z: By the same authority that they do; and I will therefore allow them to have some of it, and take the rest to myself.

Y: Are you then not aware that your generosity, which you think it your duty to bestow, would all fall on some, and that the suffering ones would suffer as much as if you did not act so?

Z: That is true; but otherwise I must perish myself, and give up my own right entirely: is this requisite?

Y: Why must any of them do so? It seems, according to your theory, that they have the most right to the ground, because they are born there, and are only passive or negative in remaining in it; but when you take it away, it is by your own voluntary action.

Z: I deny that my action in taking the ground, is really a positive one (see Definitions 1 and 2), as far as it relates to the animals in the ground; as the design (without with positive *action* of the mind cannot exist) is not on the destruction of the animals, and totally unconnected with them, but only on the ground itself. And it seems that I have as much right to preserve my life, and with a necessary degree of comfort, by disturbing the ground from without, as they have to preserve theirs by disturbing the ground within, and by debarring me of its use, to deprive me of my life. If, then, I cause

109

the destruction of some, it at least appears as just as for them to cause mine. Though even in this I may not be right, still it is a very different kind of an act to that of killing with design.

Y: I do not know that it *is* so very different; because if you kill an animal to eat it, you do not then do it with design on the life, but on the body, which is not more necessary to constitute life, than food and habitation.

Z: I admit it as an axiom, that every animal has more right to the use of its own body than others have to use it. If this principle be disbelieved, murder, and every other crime, must continually prevail. But, with regard to the ground, though I may not have more right to it, I have at least as much.

Y: What are your opinions concerning the propriety of using silk?

Z: I disapprove of the act of depriving the living grubs of their silk. I however understand, that numbers of them generally die naturally while enclosed in their silk; also that the silk of these is the most esteemed; and this of course may be used. Though I am averse to the act of depriving the living ones of their natural clothing, and substituting bran in its stead; but I severely censure the usual mode of baking them to death in an oven.

Y: Do you bear in mind, that in breeding the silkworms, we cause more to come into existence than would otherwise be the case?

Z: Though I think we are unauthorized to destroy or prevent life, life does not appear so desirable that we should perform any action for the sole purpose of producing it. Man does not possess sufficient knowledge, to do either act with design.

Y: Do you judge it wrong to use sheep's wool?

Z: I consider it an act of great cruelty to deprive the sheep of their wool, which they require themselves; which they show so keenly to feel the loss of; and which is of the same necessity to them, as clothing, shelter, beds, and the warmth of firing to us. I am, however, not so strict in my personal aversion to use wool, because my chief necessity in wearing the cloth is caused by the fashion imposed on me by others; under the pain of losing my natural place in society, and of causing the same evil to my family, by my abstaining from it. And, as there would be sufficient wool from dead sheep, if not killed, for my use, I do not positively encourage the act of shearing them alive, by purchasing the cloth. If others will not suffer the wool to remain on the sheep while living, the fault is theirs.

Y: Oh! If you reason thus, to serve your own purpose, every one else may do the same; and in what does your conduct in this respect differ from that of others?

Z: In the circumstance of my feeling strong conviction that it is only the actions of others, and the laws they impose on me to use the wool for clothing, that cause me to act so; and that for my own purpose I should be contented with the smaller quantity of what come from the dead sheep, or even without that.

Y: In what does this case differ from using meat? Does not the same apply?

Z: If even I have not a right to use the wool, it is a fault of a different description to what it would be to purchase the meat of an animal which had been killed, excepting in the case of having first proved to myself that I would prefer unslaughtered meat; because it is not done for any real necessity of my own, but is caused by the misconduct of others.

It, secondly, differs in the magnitude of the consequence.

Thirdly, there is also a difference arising from this circumstance, that one of the objects of abstaining from animal food, is to add another proof that life can be supported without, which is not applicable to the use of wool, no one doubting that it might be dispensed with.

And fourthly, it differs, because it is unlikely to make any variation in the supply of wool, whether some abstain from it or not, the whole number of sheep being shorn by all farmers every season, be the demand greater or less; because, were this not done, the farmer would suffer the loss of those crops of wool which he might leave on the sheep's back. This does not apply to the meat: as the greater the demand, the greater would be the slaughter; though perhaps not in simple proportion to it.

Y: But do you not encourage the act in the eyes of the world?

Z: I hope that I show sufficiently by my general conduct, that it is not my wish to do so.

Y: Would you deprive a sheep of its wool by your own personal act or orders?

Z: No; unless I had reason to think that the sheep would be benefited, or at least not injured, by it.

Y: Do you not think that they owe their wool to us for defending them from wolves?

Z: Certainly not, if we kill them ourselves instead of the wolves. And even were we not to kill them, we should have their bodies when they died, as a compensation. Besides, when it is considered that the defence we afford them is partly an accidental circumstance arising out of our action of defending ourselves from wolves; and partly for the purpose of saving their bodies and skins for our own use, they cannot be considered as very great debtors to us.

Y: But *we* have the trouble of defending ourselves and them also, while *they* receive their protection for nothing: would they not then, still owe something to us?

Z: If they should (from what I have alluded to), it would be but trifling: but it is very questionable if they would own any thing; for suppose C by his exertions procures his own good, and some overplus, which he leaves; and D, being helpless, takes the overplus for himself; this would not, I think, be generally considered to constitute him a debtor; much less that the debt should be so great, as for him to strip himself of his very clothing to defray it: particularly as, in the case of the sheep and the man, the latter can do very well without the wool.

Y: Suppose we were careless about possessing the bodies of the dead sheep, but that we only wished to have their wool, while living, and to give them our protection in return, by which exchange the sheep should be the gainers; would it still be unjust?

Z: I will grant that it would not, if our protection were directed to them, and not arising simple from the actions we should perform independently of them.

Y: Do they not owe something to us for their turnips, and their shelter which we afford them?

Z: Do we not owe something to them for our cutting down their forests, which would yield them food and shelter? It is also to be recollected, that in many respects they suffer greatly from being domesticated; the animal termed a moufflou, which is supposed to be a wild sheep, being a strong, an active, and a bold animal; and the very wool that we think fit to deprive sheep of, being an additional provision of nature, in our climate, apparently to protect them from its rigour.

CHAPTER VIII

On the use of vegetables; and manner of cooking them.

———

Y: Why do you not object to the use of vegetables? Perhaps they are also endowed with feeling: many naturalists are of that opinion.

Z: Perhaps they are; and *they* should, therefore, not be destroyed wantonly. But we have no sign of their having sensation, that can convince us of the fact.

Y: Do not the sensitive plants give indications of it?

Z: Probably these have sensation; but others do not evince such signs.

Y: Are we not to judge of others from them, by analogy?

Z: That is undecided.

Y: As you talk against the system of slaughtering animals for food, do you not conceive those persons who use animal food to be very guilty?

Z: It appears to me that they are not justified in so doing; but that their act in purchasing and using animal food, which had been slaughtered without their orders, is a much lighter description of wrong, than when they cause the death of the animal by their own hands or orders; and particularly when the latter acts concern graminivorous or herbaceous animals. I have also to observe, that the complexion of all actions takes its cast from the motive of the performer; that even crimes themselves, committed through an erroneously virtuous intention, are more amiable than good actions proceeding from unworthy incentives; and I should have a higher opinion of a man who should cause the destruction of everything within his power, if he conceived it to be his duty, than of another who should perform the greatest acts of kindness and real benefits to others, merely through the hope of reward.

Y: What vegetables do you conceive to be the most nutritious and agreeable?

Z: I consider wheat to be one of the first importance. This grain not only constitutes a substantial food, but is capable of producing a great variety. The different ways of using it seem almost entirely to alter its nature and qualities. When made into bread, it is one substance; into biscuits another. When used for boiled and baked pastry, two others are the result. When bread is soaked, and made into a pudding, a fifth substance is produced; all essentially different in their effects on the constitution; which each modification suits best with at different times. Fresh barley seems to be the next grain, and superior to rice, which I should judge to be inferior to many kinds of vegetable food. The best green vegetables and roots, I consider to be the different species of brassica; consisting of broccoli, cauliflowers, etc.; and the inside leaves of young cabbages: also, peas, real artichokes, potatoes, asparagus and mushrooms. It seems to me that other vegetables are not equal to these. But turnips, spinach, parsnips, etc., are also good in turn. Carrots and beetroot I should pronounce to be among the worst.

But the cooking of vegetables is not well understood. Much attention is necessary in the choosing, and in the manner of dressing them; most vegetables having but a very short time allowed them, when they may properly be said to be good, and during which they are much more wholesome and nutritious than either before or afterwards. The length of time of their boiling is very essential; it should, in my opinion, be much greater than what is commonly allowed; and enough to prevent any kind of crispness; but not more, as then the organization will be destroyed, and the water will intrude itself in their substance. Cabbages and cauliflowers should be broken into small pieces, before boiled, to prevent insects from being in them; which operation also improves their quality. They should be boiled fast in sufficient water, and well skimmed: but potatoes should boil slowly. I consider sugar, and chocolate, at times to be very nourishing. But olive oil is one of the articles of most importance in a vegetable diet. It should be used fresh in most cases. This substance seems to approach nearer to animal food than any other. It is a good substitute for butter and fat in pastry, and in frying different vegetables, as mashed potatoes, etc. Many good dishes may be made with vegetables, as soups and stews; and, by a proper application of the art of cookery, they may be rendered agreeable, though perhaps requiring more skill in the cook than animal food does. A very good soup is to be made by stewing barley with endive, turnips, parsley, celery and other vegetables.

Y: What drink do you think should be used? Are you not of opinion that much wine, malt liquor, and spirits, would be necessary when much exertion was required?

Z: Some constitutions might find them necessary; but water is the beverage most suited to mine, and particularly when there is any fatigue to undergo; though the other beverages may sometimes be good in small quantities.

CHAPTER IX

The right or the injustice of using horses contested.

———

Y: WHAT are your opinions concerning the propriety of man's compelling horses, and other beasts of burden, to perform his labour?

Z: That at least in the present state of society, it is unjust. And, considering the unnecessary abuse they suffer from being in the power of man, I think it wrong to use them, and to encourage their being placed in his power.

Y: Still it perplexes me to conceive that it can be wrong to use them with discretion: they appear to enjoy their work as well as their masters.

Z: It does not, I understand, perplex you to conceive that it can be wrong to compel slaves to work: and I am at a loss how you can disapprove of the one, and countenance the other, which appears to me to be so similar. Slaves would also at times prefer working to being kept confined.

Y: Men would work for themselves, if not made slaves of, but horses would not; and they require our authority and guidance to cause them to perform work for our benefit, and for their own.

Z: Horses, in their natural state, would perform all the work they required, in travelling about in quest of forage and shelter.

Y: But are not domesticated horses happier than wild ones? Are they not better provided with food, shelter, protection and attendance? See the account of their wild state explained here.

Z: And compare it with their domestic state, as is here also shown; which in my opinion is much worse.

Y: The sufferings of domestic horses, etc., are there shown in strong colouring; while it would far exceed the limits of our discourse, and of our powers, to enter into the various states of suffering in man. Can you compare the mere bodily pain that a horse endures, with the infinite variety of hardships, degradations, and difficulties, which the human mind has to encounter? What does a horse know of the difficulty of providing for himself and family? Of a character to lose? Of managing difficult concerns? Of being brought before a court of justice? Of being despised by his inferiors? Of uneasiness for his fate, or for those connected with him? Even the fear of death does not intrude in their minds: what they suffer is only for the moment. And, in a military campaign, can their sufferings be compared to those of the men? Even if they are cowards, they will never be brought to a court-martial. What do they know of the hardships of the life of a sailor? And from how many other evils does their ignorance protect them?

Z: I agree that there are many evils which they are unacquainted with; but also that in some cases it is owing to their being too much depressed to feel them. If they have not the difficulties of managing similar concerns to those of mankind, they have no advantage to expect from them. And if they have no court of justice or court-martial to fear, it is because their fates are in the hands of worse judges; and apparently because they experience greater evils than those which men only *dread* to experience. Besides, how do you know that they have no forethought, and no fear of death? There is scarcely any animal which shows so much timidity as the horse; while they have the same dangers to share, and greater hardships than the soldiers, and have not, after they are over, a home to retire to, and a family to comfort them.

Y: Then what is to be done with all our horses? Are they

to keep possession of the land too, to feed on, which if cultivated only by our labour, to save them the trouble, would yield but a scanty pittance to support us in performing the work of horses? And where then is *their* food to grow?

Z: They have a claim to some of the ground, as well as ourselves; and we have then only to enclose our own share.

Y: But I insist on it, that their share, or even the whole of the uncultivated ground, would not yield enough to keep them from starving.

Z: Recollect that their dung would enrich their share of the ground.

Y: What! Are we to be deprived of that too? We should have fine vegetables left to live on then, indeed!

Z: Do you think we stand in great need of it?

Y: Undoubtedly. What will grow without dung?

Z: Then, let us take some, if we can give them its equivalent, by husbanding their ground for them, and causing it to produce as much as it would do *with* all their dung, and without our care.

Y: Why is man, after having generously allotted part of the ground to their use, to have the trouble of fencing his own share, to save it from their incursions? And why should not the horse assist him in doing it, or repay him in some other way?

Z: For this slight trouble, man would have the choice of the ground; the fencing only being the landmark of distinction, partly between man and man, and partly between man and other animals. However, suppose C and D wished to divide some ground between themselves, would not C have the most chance of being a gainer, by having the choice of his share, and to fence it round, although he might wish to act with justice?

Y: Permit me to ask, then, what should be done, if it were found that horses and other cattle did really increase too fast? (In spite of your supposing that they may be so constructed as only to increase in some kind of proportion to their destruction).

Z: I don't know; this is a difficulty which we are not yet placed under. Neither do I know what should be done if mankind should increase beyond a certain limit. Perhaps, in the former case, some of the horses in England, and some other countries, might be transported to Arabia, etc., where they are wild, and from whence they were taken.

Y: Then would you have ships equipped, and sailors' lives ventured, for the sake of horses?

Z: That is not necessary; they might take the place of some articles of less importance, and which now bring in less value than the exportation of horses would save: unless we were to destroy them instead, which we should be unjust in doing.

Y: Such a commodity would take up too much room.

Z: Then, as the advantage would extend to man, he must put up with that inconvenience, if he should wish to get rid of them; and this would at least be as reasonable as to run those dangers, and incur those expenses, to obtain pearls, indigo, and other trifles.

Y: Besides, wild horses would not permit tame ones to dwell amongst them.

Z: The tame ones might herd together.

Y: How can man do without the aid of horses?

Z: That is his business to find out.

Y: Do you not think that mankind would be very miserable without their assistance?

Z: Not much more so than with it: in some cases less.

Y: That is absurd. Where are men, particularly when badly fed, to get the strength and speed of horses from for ploughing and travelling? Husbandry would then fail to produce your vegetables. Trade would cease; and mankind would become a set of ignorant and miserable beings, while their chief knowledge would extend but to a few miles from their huts. How slow would be their progress in works of art!

How little would the stimulus of emulation animate their feeble efforts! They would have enough to do to procure their most urgent necessities, and to contest with beasts of prey. By your system, they would nearly be deprived of wool, and in many places they would most likely know little of either cotton or flax; they would consequently be destitute of clothing, and even of paper. How would the situation of the English, in particular, differ from what it is, if deprived of the means of trading! Owing so many of their articles of subsistence and prosperity to foreign countries. The very cause itself of mercy towards brutes, would suffer by the ignorance that would ensue. How careful should we be, before we expose our visionary impressions, arising in the dreams of retirement, to the uninformed, to lead them astray; or the experienced, for them to laugh at! Such ideas, it is true, will enter in the mind of every thinking being, and are no novelty to them; but the discreet will treat them with mistrust. And when he sees the appearance of error in systems which have been the care of ages to mature, he will rather let them remain, than meddle with works that are far beyond his powers of investigation.

Z: What appears absurd to you, may also be owing to the want of the reflection of retirement. Are you not aware, that in most works of nature and of art, there are different modes of doing the same thing? And does it follow, because we have fixed on one means of producing it, that no other method exists? It is true that we have adopted the method of employing horses to perform our labour, by which we have most probably only chosen one method out of a great many, and we have remained contented with it. Had this not been the case, is it proved that the invention of man would not have supplied their place? Even now, you see that steam engines begin to perform in their stead. Perhaps gunpowder, and other combustibles, will supply the place of steam. A simple means also exists of causing men to draw very great weights, without employing any of the mechanical powers, which consists in using drawing poles and spikes (see the sequel). Various means have been devised, and have succeeded, of procuring more continued speed in journeys, than can be obtained from any horses, without changing; but which, from want of encouragement, and prejudice, have not become general.[1] In many places trade and communication might also exist by means of canals, without them; and there even seems little doubt that wind, or some other power, might be advantageously applied for ploughing. Besides, many of the purposes for which horses are now used, are for things of comparatively trifling importance; or for war; or for the barbarous purposes of hunting, racing, and the like; or for the rich, to show their pomp; or for strong and healthy persons, to encourage sloth and disease; and not very infrequently, for persons to get their necks and limbs broken. I grant that, without their aid, civilization might have been retarded, but not prevented. Can you suppose that your observations are new to me? And are not many improvements discovered by the force of great necessity? You may say, this change would be too dangerous an experiment. But desperate diseases require bold attempts: and were we to admit as granted, that all established customs are built with the united skill of the most experienced and wise, we should justly suffer for our timidity, and no improvements would ever be made.

Information must be gained by real intercourse with the

[1] The *velocipede* being one example of it, particularly when furnished with my addition for increasing its speed; which is described in the Repertory of Arts, vol. xxxix. June 1821; following the description of some kind of *scapers*, or substitutes for carriage wheels, for escaping obstacles, and saving labour. The same consisting of improvements on my patent, also described in the Repertory, vol. xxvi. March 1815, which is there explained; with my substitutes for cog wheels, for communicating different kinds of motion; the subject of the scapers, with some further plans of the same, being intended to be continued here, or to be directed to in some other work in which it may appear.

world, but it must be contemplated in retirement: and when we view scenes of life, as pieces of architecture, while we are in the midst of them, we see the near part too large, and the distant part too small; we must retire to a distance, to observe it all together; otherwise distortion will appear where the symmetry is just.

What causes you to think the services of horses so important to man is, that you take things as they are; *horses being used*; and you picture to yourself, that every inconvenience would be suffered, were they not used, that would be the case with an individual who should abstain from the advantage of their services, while others did not. At present every thing is adapted to ourselves, while many of the purposes of life are effected by means of the labour of horses; but were we without their assistance, and other contrivances adopted instead, then every other relative thing would be made suitable to those contrivances, and the evil which appears before you, would not seem so great. But, to the question: have you any further arguments to justify the act?

Y: Are you certain that the science of mechanics would supply every necessity for horses? I will venture to assert, that heavy commodities could not well be transported expeditiously in hilly countries, without horses, etc., by any mechanical contrivances we have an idea of.

Z: Perhaps not. We must then, for important commodities, put our own shoulders to the wheel, and effect our purpose by the force of numbers. These numbers might then occasionally consist of that part of society, who being possessed of health, strength, and property, would not refuse to work, through a mistaken idea of labour being beneath their dignity: also of the numerous and useless servants, whom they employ to wait upon them: also of the number of artisans engaged in making them beautiful clothes, magnificent houses, carriages, and other things which produce some trifling enjoyment: also of every gardener, helper in their stables, whipper-in, running footmen, etc., etc., and besides these, of poor workmen, such as those who are now dropping for want of employment, or are confined to too close application to sedentary ones.

Y: Then you would have men of rank, and artisans of every kind, occasionally harnessed to a plough or a coal-waggon, like so many beasts of burden?

Z: Yes; and include myself among the number.

Y: Are you not an admirer of the different works of art and science which grace the present age? And would they not suffer by it?

Z: I am a very great admirer of them, but not at the expense of humanity; and I consider these, and the fine arts themselves, as the last polish of a production which would be thrown away on bad or unfinished workmanship, or would perhaps, as is there the case, show the imperfections and inequalities which lie concealed when left in the rough state, and not smoothed over.

I further confess, that the great perfection to which every kind of work is brought, does not always create feelings of pure admiration in me, considering how the whole lives of human beings are devoted to one comparatively trifling purpose, to the neglect of their morals, their education, their health, and their happiness. (See Mr. Owen's remarks on this subject).

Y: Then you would impose on them hard labour also?

Z: Not also, but instead of part of their own work; and the change would frequently be of service to them, though in some cases it would of course be improper.

Y: It would be bad for business to be thus interrupted.

Z: I do not mean to enforce this as a law, but only as a custom; and when important business should intervene to one person, assistance from others might be procured. Men then would not have to complain, justly or unjustly, of there being no work for them to do.

Y: Admitting all your odd notions to be correct, granting that ships, sailors, gentry, men of science, and artisans, should all be set in motion to perform the work of horses, and that, notwithstanding all our reasoning, they should over-run us and themselves, would not their misery and their destruction, as well as our own, be the consequent end of such a wise scheme? And would not the whole creation be a victim to this project? I admit that much misery to brutes exists at present, but is it not better that some suffer, than that they should all?

Z: If this should be the case, which is far beyond our power to say would be, the evil might work its own cure, and the number of animals would most likely get reduced by famine and by disease; thus also sacrificing part to save the rest (as you observe of the present plan), and without our arbitrarily fixing on those which are to be the favoured ones. And though the whole number of animals might suffer from the overstock, their sufferings, it seems, would be less than what we constantly inflict on them. I agree that we should then share in the evil, but why should we not?

Y: You seem to take up the cause of using horses, with more earnestness than you do even the slaughtering of animals.

Z: I grant that I do, because the necessity is less; and because I conceive it worse to render a being unhappy during its whole life, than to kill it.

Y: I am as averse as you are to ill-treat animals, which is too frequently practised; but I repeat that I am not averse to use them with discretion. They were plainly designed for our service; and when well treated, they are generally attached to their masters. *They* add to his comfort; *he* to theirs.

Z: Even allowing that they are frequently well used; in sanctioning the act of subjugating them to the power of man, by the example of using them ourselves, we sanction a cause which generally leads to their misery; and though we personally give examples of kinder usage to them, we still fail not to sanction their being placed in the power of men, who in their conduct towards brutes show little disposition to imitate good examples.

Recollect what they suffer by it, even those that are the best off. Consider their treatment. Examine the whips and the spurs with which they are continually chastised while they are at work; and just try them on your own back and limbs, and on parts that have been bruised, sprained, and lacerated by previous ill-usage: feel their fluted bits in your own mouth, or only their tight girding round your body; in this plight, then exert your strength proportionably to what they do, and being besides frequently half starved, you may then reason about the state they are in.

It is the case here, as well as it is considering mankind, that we are much too apt to picture the state of each other better than it really is: little are we disposed to enter into the complaints of human beings, much less of brutes; and hard is it to have our lots in the hands of those who are ignorant of our feelings.

Y: Can you compare the thin and delicate skin of a human being, to the thick, tough hide of a horse, an ass, or an ox? Of which our shoes are made; the very soles being only the skin of an ox. What can they feel through that?

Z: Then, as you seem uniformed on this subject, I have to observe, that though their skins may be stouter than ours, animals have two skins: the first, called the scarf skin, or cuticle, is extremely thin, and nearly insensible; it is that covering which some imagine to be the only skin, and which rises in blisters. This does not compose the leather, but is corroded away by means of lime, etc., before the cutis, or true skin, is united with the substance called tannin, contained in oak bark, which then constitutes leather. The cutis, when untanned, is thick and soft, and in some places of great substance, even in the human subject. It contains a great quantity of nerves, and has acute sensibility, even more so than the flesh itself; therefore, pray do not convert this delicate and susceptible part of the animal frame, into a mere callous coating of defence.

Y: As you seem so averse to employ horses, why do you use things that are procured and effected by their labour? You might as well compel them to work yourself, as to encourage others to do it.

Z: Not so, either; the things which have been effected by their labour, might have been effected by other means, and I cannot be answerable for the acts of other persons. I should wish to avoid every action that should even unintentionally encourage the deed I disapprove of, but in this imperfect state of things I cannot pretend to it; I must, therefore, as before observed, content myself with making the first step: let others follow, and then I may make another.

Y: Why do you not object to employ men to work?

Z: Men work for their own good, and not by compulsion; and I have no desire to be idle myself, therefore I do not suppose that others have, when not indisposed.

Y: Were they not to work, would you pay them the same as if they were?

Z: I would not give them my labour, or the produce of it, for nothing; though I think that every man has a right to a share of ground, and to some of the fruits of the labour of his forefathers; but this will lead us from our subject. Yet I am further of opinion, that it is the duty of every person of property to exert himself, according to his power and abilities, for the benefit of others; and then, in accepting of their labour, we give them our own in return. But we are not to compel men to work for us, neither.

Y: If you would withhold their means of subsistence, you would compel them just in the same manner as by the stroke of a whip.

Z: No; their own necessity compels them, not mine.

Y: Well, then, the necessity of the horse to avoid the whip, is his own necessity.

Z: Arising out of his master's act of injustice. But this does not apply to a man, whom you pay by giving an equivalent, which you do not to a horse; if it be admitted that a horse be worse off in consequence.

Y: I will not admit it; but think to the contrary.

Z: Then, as their comparative states of happiness are only matter of opinion, we can neither of us tax the other with want of argument on this point. But recollect, that self-interest acts with you, and against me; and I beg you not to compare the work of horses to the work of man; the latter being simply work, while that of the horse may be considered like the employment of a soldier who is running the *gauntlet*. Even the way by which the master generally conveys his orders to the horse, is not through the medium of his proper organs of sense; seldom by conveying to his mind sounds through his ears, or light through his eyes, but by conveying pain through his nerves; by inflicting injuries on the most susceptible parts of his body; and this is almost the only language by which his orders for increased exertion are given to him.

Y: It is to be recollected, that horses frequently draw punishment on themselves by their perverseness: I have frequently seen them refuse to go in some particular road, and obstinately persevere to turn into another, as if only from a spirit of contradiction.

Z: So it may appear at first sight, but one moment of attention to the case will even point out the true cause generally of this, and soon will it occur to the mind, that the road objected to by the horse is one charged with the terrors of previous chastisement received in it.

I have to ask, if you would approve of the act of using them, if you were of opinion that their situations were rendered worse by it?

Y: Perhaps I should, if they were not caused to suffer very much in consequence, as they might at least share the burdens of life with man; and if even they were entirely sacrificed for man, it would only be an inferior thing spent to save a superior.

Z: What has one being to do with another?

Y: Do you not say, that equality of good and evil should exist between two beings?

Z: That is true, but not when it requires the performance of positive injury to render them equal.

Besides, on this principle it would be just to kill an old man to save a young man, the life to be expected by an old man being shorter, and consequently of less importance.

Y: I conclude that in some of your observations you only wish it understood, that you are *most inclined* to view things as you have expressed, and that you are not quite certain of being right.

Z: What you conclude is just.

Y: Are you sure that your opinions will always be the same?

Z: No; I am not sure that any of my opinions will always be the same.

Y: Would not the lot of mankind, under your system, be worse than that of any other animal?

Z: Why should it be? Man would still have the power in his own hands, and would always be better able to provide for his wants, than other animals could do, the former having fire, water, and all kinds of materials at his disposal, wherewith to build houses, and to make clothes, beds, and other comforts; while other animals, also possessing wants, would still be destitute of any of these advantages.

Y: Seriously, do you not think that you have overreached your mark?

Z: Possibly I may have done so, though unconscious of it; but almost the only way of reaching a difficult point, is to attempt to stretch beyond it. It is true, that I am not convinced of the right of man to slaughter other animals for food, particularly of those which subsist entirely on vegetables; but I do not tax with the slaughter, persons who only purchase and use the meat which had been slaughtered against their wish. I have not even prohibited the use of horses; but I must confess that, until the morals and dispositions of men shall be much improved, I am inclined to think it would be better for those who are kindly disposed towards them, to abstain from their services, than to sanction their subjugation to men, in the present uncultivated state of mankind.

Y: Why should you not, in difficult subjects, put some trust in the opinions of others? You cannot expect to decide them all yourself: and you must bear in mind, that you are not only opposed by the vulgar, but by far the greatest part of the most enlightened; even by many mathematicians, whose business is to solve the most intricate and abstruse questions; these concur in the opinion that man should enjoy entire dominion over every other creature, and that they were created solely for his use; still you dispute it!

Z: What you view as a circumstance in favour of your cause, I conceive to be one against it; because it seems that among all these wise men, whose wish it has been to show the justice of this, and who were so capable of proving what they asserted, not one of them has succeeded in their attempts on this subject: I therefore almost despair of finding a proof myself, and cannot even but suspect the doctrine to be fallacious, in consequence of my very respect for their general opinions: though this may be paradoxical.

Y: There are some things of which we are convinced ourselves, without our having the power to demonstrate them to others; we should, therefore, sometimes trust to the conviction of others, although they may likewise be unable to prove what they conceive to be true.

Z: Not if it appears absurd.

Y: You must not think things absurd because you cannot understand them. Why do you not conceive it absurd for there to be a power of gravity? You are also unable to account for this; still you do not dispute it.

Z: No; I cannot take any thing on trust which appears absurd; unless the proof be open to me. I believe in the power of gravity, because I see its effects; and though unable to account for it, I perceive nothing absurd in the fact. You have, I observe, fallen into a prevalent error of confounding difficulties with absurdities. The example you have brought, may contain an insurmountable difficulty, yet it bears no absurdity nor contradiction to our sense. But if, for instance, you should assert that eighteen and two did not produce twenty; or that you could place a solid figure, without altering its size or shape, into a similar space, but less than the solid figure, I should then contradict you point blank. Still I do not, in the case we have discussed, pretend that either side of the question bears the same kind of absurdity.

Y: I have only further to observe, that you frequently talk of what we have a right to do, and what not, and of justice and injustice. Can you give me a definition of justice, or of what you understand by the word?

Z: My ideas of justice are explained in the foregoing, and chiefly depend on Axiom 1, and Axiom 5.

I have now received your attacks, and have defended myself as well as I am able: how far I have succeeded, must be left to good and impartial judges. But I hope at least I have proved that a greater share of inconsistency has not fallen to my lot than has to others.

Y: Why! What inconsistency have you to charge me with? I am ready to defend myself on that point.

Z: Then I am ready to attack you; and, I think, with at least as much success as you have had in your encounter with me for the same charge.

Y: Then begin.

CHAPTER X

Z attacks Y. Defence of Y. Y denies the power of moral arguments.
Z opposes this, and gives some examples. Y asks Z to put a question
to him. Z disapproves of the answer.

Z: PERMIT me to ask you, on my part, what morals you
adopt? And what you lay down as the fundamental part of
rectitude of conduct?

Y: The fundamental part of morality by which I am
guided, consists in the endeavour to love others as well as
myself.

Z: It is true, that the more the nature of your general love
of mankind resembles the nature of self-love, the better it will
be; but the difficulty of attaining to perfection in this virtue,
and of regulating the degree as well as the nature of the love
for others, renders some other principles also necessary. You
must recollect that mankind is numerous, and do you mean
to assert, that the degree of love for them all, could equal that
which you possess for yourself?

Y: It ought to be so.

Z: But not better, I suppose?

Y: No, not better.

Z: Then, I suppose that if you and another person were in
danger, you would as soon try to save him as yourself?

Y: I ought.

Z: Suppose ten persons were with you, would you not
much rather save nine of them, than only one?

Y: Assuredly.

Z: Then, you would rather save nine of them than yourself; and if there were a very great number, yourself would become almost forgotten.

Y: Well, then I say that I should love all mankind together, as well as I do myself.

Z: Then, how much more must you love yourself, than you do one of them!

Y: That is sophistry.

Z: Do you conceive it a crime, to commit murder (on an innocent person) to save your own life?

Y: Undoubtedly.

Z: How do you know it to be a crime?

Y: We are commanded by the laws of our country, not to commit murder.

Z: Can you not prove it to be wrong, independently of this command, by the laws of morality?

Y: Yes; by our own conscience.

Z: Is this all?

Y: No; the example would be injurious.

Z: Then, if you could do it with certain secrecy, would nothing else than command and conscience prevent you?

Y: Yes; love of mankind.

Z: But I have proved to you, that love of mankind would not be so great as self-love, and therefore you would on this ground rather preserve yourself.

Y: I should consider his life of as much importance as mine.

Z: Suppose he were older than you, and of course not in expectation of such length of life as yourself, how would you do then?

Y: That requires consideration; but the command, and my conscience, would be my guide.

Z: Give me further to understand, of what you consider virtue and vice chiefly to consist, as far as it relates to conduct to others.

Y: In having a regard for the welfare of others; in keeping the laws which have been, or which ought to have been enacted for public good; and even to sacrifice myself for them; because I judge that the importance of numbers is more than that of an individual; (though I do not infer that it is necessary to do myself a great injury, to cause a trifling public good). This is the basis upon which the laws of all countries are founded and observed.

Z: What do you conceive to be your first duty in affairs concerning mankind and other animals?

Y: First, to take care of myself and family, without infringing the laws of public good: after that, follows the performance of good to others, in proportion to their proximity to myself, and to their wants.

Z: Would you do injury to another, to do yourself as much good?

Y: No; the example would cause a public evil.

Z: Why so? If the act itself be not bad, repetition (under the same circumstances) cannot be bad.

Y: Yes; the *knowledge* of the insecurity resulting, would destroy society.

Z: Then, if you were certain of secrecy, would it be bad notwithstanding?

Y: Perhaps not; but we could not be certain.

Z: It seems then, that it is not the immediate consequence of the crime that prevents you from committing it, but chiefly that which follows it. What would your associates think of you, if they know that you would injure them secretly, in order to do yourself good?

Y: I would not injure them so as to render myself worse off than myself, but only so as to render myself equally happy with them.

Z: Well, I am glad you admit of my axiom, that all beings should be equally happy; but how could you tell which were happier or less happy than yourself?

Y: I could not be certain, but would judge from appearances.

Z: Suppose you were suffering pain, and another was enjoying pleasure, would you secretly, to ease your own sufferings, destroy the enjoyment of the other?

Y: Perhaps so.

Z: Then if the case were reversed, should you not destroy your own enjoyment, to prevent pain to the other?

Y: Yes; it would at least be a debt.

Z: But you would most probably not be present; and you would then be unable to discharge your debt.

Y: Still, if this plan were general, some one else would pay him, and I would pay another instead; and by the laws of chance, we should all become paid in time.

Z: Suppose this should not become general, then certain evil to the other would ensue, in being deprived of his enjoyment; as we must not only look at the present, but every one must have his holiday in turn.

Y: Then, with those considerations, I would not act so; as the share of pleasure and pain of one individual, should equal that of another.

Z: How could you know when you had less than your share, and when you had more?

Y: I would judge to the best of my abilities.

Z: I think you would have very little idea.

Y: Well, then you admit of the necessity of equality of happiness as well as I do; therefore you would in this case act the same as I should do myself, and if that be inconsistent, you share in *my* inconsistency, while I do *not* in *yours*; therefore you are still the greatest defaulter, on the ground of inconsistency.

Z: That is because my doctrine embraces much of yours also; and of course the more extended any thing is, the more numerous will generally be the imperfections: however, I understand you conceive it to be a crime to be dishonest; prove it to be so.

Y: It is an axiom, that if any thing belongs to one person, no other person has a right to take it away from him.

Z: What right have you to property more than others?

Y: I worked for part; and the other part has been given to me.

Z: Perhaps your work was not worth more than the work that others receive less for; and what right had any one to the part he gave you? Are you certain that any person has a right to more than his share, because he possesses the fortune or the skill to obtain it? Is there not any difference between such laws as what have been made by nations, and real justice? Recollect that though the latter should be attended to, not any moralist will be satisfied by only observing such laws, as were by wise men judged practicable, in the management of the general affairs of society in the *gross*. Much praise, however, is due to those, who have established the laws which have rendered us as well off as we are; though every person knows they are unavoidably imperfect, and hopes for their amendment. But, can you prove dishonesty, in the general acceptation of the word, to be a crime, independently of its infringement of the laws?

Y: Honesty must always be practised according to the general idea of what honesty consists of; and when this is not done, general disorder ensues.

Z: It appears, then, that you have not any idea of crime in itself, but only when the thing becomes general?

Y: Yes; the gifts of providence should be equally divided, according to the wants of every one.

Z: This is my opinion also; but wants are unequal. How are we to know the wants of others correctly?

Y: Every one should have an equal share.

Z: Perhaps that would be the most just; but it would fall far short of real justice, and very hard on those who required more.

Y: That would be their misfortune.

Z: And are you sure that there would then be less evil,

than when managed in any other manner?

Y: I think so.

Z: But you are very far from being sure, and cannot prove it.

Y: We must do our best; we cannot do any more.

Z: Are you sure that you would be morally right, in *retaining* more property than came to your share?

Y: More than my share! I must consider.

Z: You seem hard pressed. Then I will answer for you: That, generally, a person would be wrong in so doing, though particular occasions may render it right; for instance, when it was retained as a compensation for some other evil, or for objects of benefit to others. It seems necessary for us both to make a distinction between positive and negative acts; otherwise we must go into greater obscurities.

It further appears to me, that positive crimes are the worse, and should be fastidiously avoided: also, that it is better to abstain from acts of positive good to some, than to perform them, if positive evil and crime must in consequence be committed on others. I should, therefore, prefer that individual, who exerted his forbearance in abstaining from evil, though deficient in the virtue of attempting to promote the good of others, to him who pursued the object of ameliorating the condition of some, and inflicted unjust sufferings on others; because, a person who does good to one, and harm to another, changes the state of happiness and misery between them; and this being an undue authority. It may appear strange, though not less the fact, that the very contradictory traits of disposition, of doing good and evil, frequently occur together in the same person, to a very great extent; numerous examples being found of men who would brave any danger to preserve the life of another person; and who would also, in other respects, be guilty of the greatest atrocities.

In short, our *first* duty seem to be, *to do as little harm as possible*. The *second* duty - *to do good*. It also appears, that one innocent being must not be injured for the benefit of another; at least where the injury is of magnitude; and more particularly when the benefit is not very great. The difficulty to ourselves, in attending to either the negative or the positive case, must also be considered; and we are not to expect to attain to the greatest negative perfection, before we attempt an act of positive good. I hope, however, that you will now withdraw your charge of inconsistency, or submit to the same tax yourself.

Y: If even I am inconsistent, it is no excuse for your being so.

Z: And if my morals *are* inconsistent, why should I change them for others possessing the same fault? You seem unable to give any decided reasons for abstaining from committing the greatest crimes, without those reasons leading you into absurdities. You first say, that you should love all mankind as you do yourself; whereby your love for another, and for yourself, will both be very small, as you have many claimants amongst whom to share your regard. Besides, you would then be incapable of forming any more friendship for your relatives and associates, than for strangers. Afterwards, you assert it to be your duty, to do good to your relatives and friends first; why then should *this* be?

I agree with you, that were our dispositions perfect, we should all be friends alike: but here we must both forgo this claim to perfection, and content ourselves with coarser fare. I am persuaded that no principle of morality will bear our close investigation without showing some flaws; but we must embrace that which is of the *greatest extension*, provided the imperfections be not *proportionately* greater than those of other principles which are less extended.

Y: Will you not say, that we should love all mankind as we do ourselves?

Z: In cases of absolute right and wrong, we must not let self-love interfere; and we should also possess the same *kind* of love for all mankind, as we do for ourselves; but the *degree* cannot be expected to equal that of self-love.

Y: I think that you attempt to treat moral subjects in too formal and in too methodical a manner: you pretend to decide questions which will not bear actual demonstration (as not any moral subject can) with the air of a mathematician in proving a real truth. I ask you, if you can prove, in any one of your arguments, what you endeavour to do, as well as that the three angles of every triangle are equal to two right angles?

Z: I own that I wish to imitate and to follow the method of a mathematician, and am of opinion that some moral arguments are nearly as conclusive as mathematical ones, which they may in fact almost be considered; for instance, the argument, as it would stand from natural causes, concerning the will of an animal. I will, however, give you another example:

That the idea of there being any disease which is entirely hereditary is erroneous, unless that the disease can by no other means be produced than from parent to offspring; and provided that those persons who are afflicted with it, be equally capable with others of becoming parents.

For suppose a parent, having any disease, communicates it to his children; let the number of his children be four, or any other number; then each of these four must by hypothesis have the disease; and in order to allow for the continuance of the human race, we must suppose that two of the children will become parents in their turn, and in like manner communicate the disease to their offspring, so as continually to keep up the same proportion of the disease as existed at first. But if the disease can be propagated in any other way, there will be continually additions made to the number of diseased; and in the course of time, the whole race of mankind would be subject to this disease; which is absurd to suppose. It is also evident, that the number would increase still faster, as only one of the parents having the disease was supposed to be sufficient.

Y: Ask me a moral question, and I will solve it.

Z: Suppose you were possessed of a certain sum of money, say £1,000; and your only son, being in pecuniary distress, should beg £100 of you, which you, in virtue of your *affection* for him, should grant: but suppose he, having had the misfortune to be robbed of the £100 (without its having been owing to any fault or peculiarity of situation in him), should again come to you for assistance; what sum would you give him then?

Y: Perhaps none; because I should have done my duty before.

Z: Then, you would act so as to perform your duty, and not from affection. Would you love him the less, because you had assisted him?

Y: But I must take care of myself too.

Z: So you might have said at first. Why should you have given him any thing?

Y: Because I possessed affection for him; though not sufficient to ruin myself.

Z: Then, you mean to say, that a man possessed of £1,000 should give £100, and a man possessed of £900 should give nothing?

Y: Not if he had given him his due before. It is just for a father to assist his son to a certain amount, but not more.

Z: I agree with you, as far as your duty is concerned; but the laws of affection are different: and if C gives any thing to D, in virtue of his affection for him, the gift should be governed by a comparison of the wants of them both, without any attention to what he had already ineffectually given him.

Y: I understand you to be of opinion, that the quantity of good or evil between two beings, during their whole existence, should be equal: therefore, if C had given some of his good away already, in order to render his share equal to that of D, by giving a second time, his own share might become deficient.

Z: But in the case of affection, the good of C would be derived from the good of D.

Y: A person may have affection for another, and still prefer his own advantage to theirs.

Z: Then he should not have given him the first time.

Y: Well, how do *you* think C ought to act?

Z: That depends on the nature of their wants: and if in the first instance he had given him a tenth, the second time he should give a tenth of the remainder; and the third time in the same proportion; and so for the rest. Though the sum of money must not be rated by its numerical value, but by the degree of good that each sum would produce to C and to D.

Y: Then C would soon ruin himself.

Z: Why so? This neither proves that C should give more nor less; but that the sum which *he does* give, should be managed in that manner; unless the situation of C should become too much distressed to preserve or to attend to his affection for D.

CHAPTER XI

Mr. Martin's Act, with observations on it.

―――

JUDGING that some persons may be desirous of information on what has lately been done by our Legislature in the cause of humanity, we have here to subjoin an abstract, or abridgement, of Mr. R. Martin's Act on this subject; though, as it appears, mutilated, as might have been foretold, from the numerous lovers of cruelty who have opposed it. We shall, however, in giving the substance of the Act, and in hoping for its speedy amendment, also take the liberty of adding some observations, and of pointing out some slight alterations, which it seems would accord with the intention of the Act, and be productive of beneficial results.

Abstract or abridgement of the Act we have alluded to, and referring to the prevention of the cruel and improper treatment of cattle: dated the 22nd of July, 1822.

Item 1, Expresses, that if any person shall wantonly and cruelly (see Note 1) beat, abuse, or ill-treat any horse, mare, gelding, mule, ass, ox, cow, heifer, steer, sheep, or other cattle, and complaint on oath thereof be made to any justice of the peace, or other magistrate, within whose jurisdiction such offence shall be committed, it shall be lawful (see Note 2) for such justice of the peace, or other magistrate, to issue his summons or warrant, at his discretion, to apprehend them; and shall examine upon oath any witness, and shall on conviction by his own confession, or upon such information as aforesaid, be subjected to a forfeit of any sum not exceeding five pounds, nor less than ten shillings, to His Majesty (see Note 3), or on refusal or inability to pay the sum forfeited, shall be committed to the house of correction, or other prison within the jurisdiction within which the offence shall have been committed, there to be kept without bail or mainprise for any time not exceeding three months.

Item 2, Expresses that no person shall be punished unless complaint be made within ten days after the offence; and any person having suffered imprisonment for such offence, shall not afterwards be subjected to a penalty for it.

Item 3, Expresses that no order or proceeding to be made or had by or before any justice of the peace, or other magistrate, by virtue of the Act, shall be quashed or vacated for want of form, and that the order of such justice or other magistrate shall be final; none of the proceedings of whom shall be removed by *certiorari* or otherwise.

Item 4, Relates to the form of conviction; in which the offence, time, and place, are to be specified, as the case may be.

Item 5, Expresses that if the justice of the peace, or other magistrate, on his hearing of such complaint, shall be of opinion that it was frivolous or vexatious (see Note 3), it shall then be lawful for him to order, adjudge and direct the complaint to pay the defendant any sum of money not exceeding twenty shillings, as compensation for his trouble and expense, such order or adjudgement to be final, and the sum to be paid and levied in the same manner as before expressed relating to offenders.

Item 6, Expresses that any action or suit *must* be commenced within six calendar months after every cause or action shall have accrued, and shall be brought, laid, and tried, in the county, city, or place, in which such offence shall have been committed, and not elsewhere; and that the defendant may plead the general issue, and give the act and the special matter in evidence at any trial to be had thereon; and that the same was done in pursuance and by authority of the act; and that if the same shall appear to have been so done, or if any such action or suit shall not be commenced within the time before limited, or shall be brought in any other country, city, or place, than where the offence shall have been committed, then the jury shall find for the defendant; or if the plaintiff shall become nonsuit, or shall discontinue his action, or if judgement shall be given for the defendant therein, then and in any of the cases aforesaid, such defendant shall have treble costs, and shall have such remedy for recovering the same, as in any other case at law.[1]

Notes and observations on such alterations as it appears would amend this Act.

Note 1. Instead of, "cruelly and wantonly" we propose to insert, cruelly *or* wantonly.
Note 2. Instead of, "it shall be lawful" we propose to insert, it is here commanded.
Note 3. Instead of, "to His Majesty" we propose to insert, half to His Majesty.
Note 4. Instead of "was frivolous or vexatious" we propose to insert, was made with frivolous or vexatious intention.

We also propose the two following Items to be added:

Item 1. That the construction, size, weight, and material of all whips, bits, spurs, harness, saddle, etc., be rendered less galling, and be appointed and limited by act of parliament, and that a tax be levied on them separately.
Item 2. That the *sides* of every carriage, cart, horse, ass, and other beast, shall bear a number, and the address of its owner; and that a fine shall be imposed when these are omitted, half of which shall go to His Majesty, and half to the informer.

[1] The whole Act may be purchased for sixpence, at the King's printer's in Gough Square, Fleet Street.

In Note 1, the substitution of the word *or* for *and* must appear necessary to every friend of humanity; and to oppose this would be an open protestation of enmity to its cause. On what grounds can opposition to this alteration rest? Is all cruelty proper which is not termed wanton? Is its necessity obvious? Is it sanctioned by good education, by religion, or by the kind of feeling we should wish those to possess who had our own fates at their disposal? Is it right that brutes should be allowed to suffer every barbarity which the most trifling purposes of their more brutal masters should exact? And that they should be permitted to plead *not guilty*, because *not wanton*?

It is true that the word *wanton* properly applies to all crimes which cause to the perpetrator more loss than profit, exclusively of the pleasure he takes in committing cruelty; yet some there are who think differently, and who would not arrogate to themselves to pronounce any acts wanton, but such as would also be admitted to be wanton by those who were desirous to misconstrue the term. Let then the scrupulous be relieved from their difficulty; let this invidious or unmeaning *and* be expunged; and then may the advantage be felt by some of the most unfortunate and most helpless of beings, who have no language to plead in, no power to reproach you with, who being ignorant of the part you take, will not molest you for injuring their cause, nor reward you for benefiting it, and who have no appeal to your feelings but that which originates without your own breasts and in your superior wisdom.

But only let this alteration be proposed, and it will, we trust, be adopted. There are men who are alive to the calls of humanity, and endowed with other qualities necessary for seconding the objects of this Bill, who, it is to be hoped, will assist in preventing its purposes from being frustrated, or turned aside, by any force or insidiousness with which they may be assailed.

The alteration of Note 2 is also necessary, in order to render the Act more effectual, and to relieve the magistrates from the responsibility of acting or not acting, and generally to facilitate its objects.

The importance of the alteration in Note 3, is too evident to need comment, and without which it is to be feared the Act will never be generally useful; there being but few persons capable and willing to take the trouble of a prosecution without some remuneration attending it.

The alteration in Note 4, is also particularly essential; because, if it be expedient to prevent the abuse, it is certainly absurd and unjust to oppose difficulties to those who are the instruments of its prevention; or to subject them to the risk of such a decision as would be formed by those who were too ready to conceive a complaint of cruelty to be frivolous - though we should be sorry to believe such a disposition at present to exist in any magistrate or justice of the peace who have to decide in these cases. Also in order to prevent this business and other business from interfering with each other, it appears that it would be expedient to have a separate department for this alone.

We should rejoice to see the two additional Items which we have proposed, subjoined to this Act; and it is to be borne in mind that if these alterations, etc., should fail of producing good, they cannot possibly do much harm; while the good they promise would not only refer to the animals themselves, but also to the possessors of their skins after their death; it being asserted that those parts of the cutis or skin of horses, etc., which have been most subjected to the action of the spurs, saddles, whips, and harness, instead of being thickened by it, as some suppose, are generally worn to such thinness and friability, as to be almost useless for any purpose.

Even to mankind the effects of this Bill, when properly amended, may be expected to be highly beneficial, as cruelty is cruelty under whatever colouring it may appear; and whether exercised on a man or on a fly, cruelty is still cruelty. It matters not whether the victim be furnished with two legs or with four, with wings, with fins, or with arms; where there is sensation, there is subject for cruelty, and in proportion to the degree of sensation will its action operate.

Cruelty, then, always being the same, how terrible must be the result of encouraging it in any instance!

It is too evident that the passion for it being once excited, soon extends itself beyond the bounds prescribed, and objects of the brute creation alone do not satisfy its craving; human beings then become the sacrifice, and tyranny and bloodshed the result.

Let us then strike at the root of that evil which is so prejudicial to man, and amend this bill: the consequence will be gratifying to the philanthropist, the philosopher and the statesman; and if the voice of the living should fail in establishing its purposes, let us dwell on the memory of him, whose virtue has lately excited the love and the admiration of all who were acquainted with the name of Erskine, and recollect that in promoting the interests of this bill we execute the *will* of our friend.

Much more remains still to say on this topic, and on cruelty to animals in general, several of its subjects not having been here treated on; but I will take advantage of referring to an excellent little work, entitled "As Essay on Humanity to Animals, by Thomas Young, A. M.," which has fallen into my hands since the foregoing has been put to press, containing many of those that have been omitted, and also corroborating several of the sentiments we have expressed.

CHAPTER XII

Vagrant Act and Tread Mills.

———

HAVING given a copious extract of the Act concerning brutes to our readers, we will not, in justice to our own species, refrain from expressing our desire to direct their attention to another Act, dated only two days later, well known by the name of the Vagrant Act; being an act for consolidating into one act and amending the laws of vagrants, etc., in England. This we are happy to say, expires the 1st of September 1824, and will not, we hope, be renewed in its present state. The act, though it certainly embraces many objects of utility, in several other instances, we are of opinion, consigns to severe punishment many unfortunate and wretched human beings, while the only fault with which they are accused, as it appears, is that of being so. It distinguishes three kinds of offenders -

The first relates to "idle and disorderly persons."
The second to "rogues and vagabonds;" and the
third to "incorrigible rogues."

Those who are deemed idle and disorderly, are made liable to be committed to hard labour in the house of correction for one month or less.

Among the offenders deemed rogues and vagabonds, are included all common stage-players acting for gain, such persons not being authorized by law; and all petty chapmen, and pedlars wandering abroad, not being duly licensed or otherwise authorized by law; and all persons wandering abroad and lodging in ale-houses, out-houses, barns, or in the open air, or under tents, or in carts, or waggons, and not giving a good account of themselves; and all other persons wandering abroad, or placing themselves in streets, etc., to beg or gather alms.

Among the numerous description of incorrigible rogues are denominated those apprehended as rogues and vagabonds and escaping, or refusing to go, and those who being charged with any offence against this Act, and being bound by recognizance as is there expressed, shall neglect to appear; and also those committed for a second offence.

It seems absolutely necessary to define what is meant by the giving a good account of themselves; and on the justice of this definition must depend the justice of the cause: but that it should be left to the power of the magistrate, is not only imposing a hard duty on him, but is a great injury to the public; and with respect to beggars, however depraved many of them may be, the inflicting punishment on them without crime having been actually proved, is certainly both cruel and unjust.

These, and all who are denominated rogues and vagabonds, are ordered to be searched, and made liable to have the money and effects which may be found on them applied for the expense of their apprehension and maintenance during the time they may be committed, returning the overplus, if any.

They are then made liable to be tried, and to be further punished as rogues and vagabonds, to be detained in the house of correction, there to be kept to hard labour for any time not exceeding six months; and incorrigible rogues for a year: and during the time of such person's confinement in both cases to be corrected by whipping (not being a female), at such times and places as according to the nature of the offence may be thought fit. And in case any such person shall have been before adjudged an incorrigible rouge, the justice may order him to be imprisoned in any common gaol or house of correction, there to be kept to hard labour for two years, and during such confinement to be further corrected by whipping, if the justice shall think fit.

But a great improvement has by some been deemed to exist in the mode of punishment to the transgressors of this act, by the introduction of the tread mills; though by others viewed as an object of serious disapprobation. However unimportant our opinion on this subject may be, we confess ourselves to be among the latter; and that whether the tread wheels be a more severe or a milder mode of treatment than that adopted before their establishment, we still cannot, in their application to these cases, consider them otherwise than as powerful engines of injustice, of cruelty, and even of slavery itself. The evils attached to them were obvious to some reflecting persons on their very first appearance; and now time, it seems, has added the test of dearly bought experience in corroboration of what they had predicted, in the injurious effects which have been authentically represented to have been produced on many of those subject to the action, particularly to females, and the serious accidents to which it renders persons liable.

In the public reports the general health of the prisoners is stated to be greatly improved by it; but with the greatest deference to the judgement of those who have declared their opinion with regard to the health of the prisoners, we should still prefer the acknowledgement of this circumstance from their own mouths. We will not however dispute that the exercise may be beneficial to some of them; admitting this, and even that in *most* cases it may be so, it cannot be denied that in *some* individuals a reverse effect takes place, or that instances may be adduced where the prisoners had begun the employment in tolerably good health, and the same having left it in a most deplorable condition, with their constitutions apparently quite ruined[1]. What right have we then in justice to subject these to such evils, merely because the generality are benefited by the exercise? While the faults for which the former are chastised, may be those requiring commiseration instead, and (as I have seen observed) because they are destitute and friendless, or perhaps because they may be, owing to a certain degree of ill-health or indisposition, rendered inactive, and unable to perform the labour necessary for their own benefit, and therefore condemned without judge or jury to labour still more, almost for nothing, reprimanded for their idleness as it is termed, and exposed to the ridicule of their associates. It has also been urged, that the longer the prisoners had undergone the punishment, the more was their health improved. But this may probably arise from their becoming more expert, and consequently using rather less exertion in their motions than

[1] Case of George Barnes - a youth aged about nineteen, who it appears had been committed as a vagrant to the tread mill at Brixton for three months, having been in good health at his commencement, and having left it in a most debilitated and sickly condition, and removed to the workhouse at Lambeth.

Part of his own account is as follows:

That he began in good health, and left in a state of sickness. That at one time he slipped off the wheel, and received severe injury. That the employment is excessively laborious. That if they should stop while the wheel was going, their legs or feet would get between the fans and would probably get fractured. That in summer their hours of work are from six to six, meals and intervals included. That sometimes they work an hour and a quarter without stopping. That they are not allowed to rest much weight on the hand rail. That if the men object to work, they are kept without food, and deprived of their beds; and boys flogged. That if they plead illness during the absence of the surgeon, their working or not rests with the turnkey. That each man has 1½ lb of bread per day, for four days in the week, and for the three remaining days, 1lb of bread, and four ounces of boiled meat per day. Bread and water for breakfast, and sometimes two or three potatoes for supper, or soup made from their meat, with vegetables not washed and full of caterpillars; that this was the whole of their diet, excepting a little gruel, and that they are not allowed to purchase or receive any other food.

they did at first. It may without offence be seriously asked, why (if the tread mill be so great a restorer of health) do not most of its advocates, when they feel themselves indisposed, submit their own persons to its influence, with the same rigour and the same diet as they prescribe, and place themselves also at the discretion of the gaoler? Or it may be further demanded, if they would wish to see those whom they highly regarded (for instance, their wives or their parents) working at this monotonous, laborious and degrading occupation? A true picture in the mind of this, would probably tend to such a decision as would be founded on a just regard of the prisoner, and we hope also on a due observance of the public good.

In all chastisements, even for the greatest crimes, equality of punishments to every individual possessing equal guilt, should be aimed at; and though this object cannot be completely attained, it must never be neglected. Bodily labour however seems more unequal in its effects than almost any other mode of correction, the same degree of labour being in some instances even a pleasure to one person, that would actually destroy another; and this may indeed in some cases be asserted of the same individual at different times. Why then should the weak or the debilitated be put to the same task as the strong and healthy? Or why should the gaoler, or even the surgeon, have the power of appropriating their work according to his own ideas of their strength? A task which no one can perform with any certainty of justice to the prisoners, the external tokens of health being only uncertain signs at best.

A machine has, we understand, been invented for a similar purpose, that can be worked either with the feet or the hands of the prisoner, so that he may choose his work according to which action he may be most able to perform. This, though far from producing equality, yet allows of more than the tread wheel; and as the powers and the dispositions of different individuals vary greatly from each other, the choice of two or three modes of receiving punishment to the prisoner would generally tend to its equality and its justice.

It is also to be recollected, that in enforcing labour as a punishment, aversion for labour is frequently produced instead of industry. The truth of this, as far as it relates to the same sort of labour, has been represented in the circumstance of a machine having been invented to be worked in the manner of a tread wheel, and from the inventor having been obliged to alter his plan, from the horror that existed in the minds of the men who were to work it, simply from the idea of the punishment it is used for.

But as the moral as well as the physical improvement of the prisoners, is professed to be among the objects of these institutions, it may be fairly asked by what means the tread mills possess the power, beyond other punishments which are equally severe, of reclaiming the wicked, and of instructing them in the paths of religion, of honesty, and of decorum? Yet, as it really seems to be the wish of its advocates to attain these objects, might it not be more favourable to their views, to cause some of the prisoners to apply their industry in receiving tuition, in reading, in writing, and in whatever might appear to increase their understanding and to improve their morals? And might it not also be feasible to erect workshops for those who were acquainted with trades, and for the teaching those who were able to learn them? Idleness might then frequently be prevented, and cruelty banished from many of our prisons.

CHAPTER XIII

Proposed Bill of Mr. Martin, to alter and amend an Act passed in the third year of the reign of His present Majesty, entitled "An Act to prevent the cruel and improper treatment of cattle."

WHEREAS by an act made in the third year of the reign of His present Majesty King George the Fourth, it is amongst other things enacted, that if any person or persons should wantonly and cruelly beat, abuse, or ill-treat any horse, mare, gelding, mule, ass, ox, cow, heifer, steer, sheep or other cattle, and complaint on oath thereof should be made to any justice of the peace, or other magistrate within whose jurisdiction such offence should be committed, it should be lawful for such justice of the peace or other magistrate to issue his summons or warrant, at his discretion, to bring the party or parties so complained of before him, or any other justice of the peace, or other magistrate of the county, city, or place within which such justice of the peace or other magistrate had jurisdiction, who should examine upon oath any witness or witnesses who should appear to be produced to give information touching such offence; and if the party or parties accused should be convicted of any such offence, he, she, or they, so convicted, should forfeit and pay the sum therein mentioned.

And whereas the provisions of the said recited act have been found insufficient to prevent the offences therein mentioned, and it is expedient to make further provision for that purpose, be it enacted by the King's Most Excellent Majesty, by and with the advice and consent of the Lords Spiritual and

Temporal, and Commons, in this Parliament assembled, and by the authority of the same, that if any person or persons shall wantonly and cruelly beat, abuse, or ill-treat any of the said herein before mentioned animals, or any other cattle, or shall overload any horse or other beast of burden, he, she, or they, shall be and be deemed guilty of a misdemeanour, and being convicted thereof, shall suffer such punishment as in other cases of misdemeanour.

And be it further enacted, that it shall be lawful for any person or persons who shall witness such offence as aforesaid, to apprehend every person so offending, and to convey such offender or offenders before any justice of the peace or other magistrate within whose jurisdiction such offence shall be committed; and it shall thereupon be lawful for such justice of the peace or other magistrate, either to commit or bail such person or persons, to be proceeded against for such misdemeanour by indictment under this act; or it shall be lawful for such justice of the peace or other magistrate to proceed against and deal with such person or persons in such manner as is provided by the said herein before recited act.

And be it further enacted, that if any justice of the peace, or other magistrate, shall witness such offence as aforesaid within his jurisdiction, it shall be lawful for him, on his view thereof, to convict and punish the party or parties so offending, in such manner as he might do, under the said herein before recited act, upon information and proof made before him of such offence.

And be it further enacted, that it shall be lawful for any justice of the peace or other magistrate, before whom any person shall be convicted under the said recited act, or under this act, to order any sum of money not exceeding of such sum as shall be awarded against the person so convicted, to be paid to the person or persons who shall prosecute such offender to conviction, as compensation for his or their trouble and expense in and about such prosecution.

Further objects of Petition Societies.

THOUGH we have already treated on Petition Societies, not having entered into the nature of many of the subjects they are wished to comprehend, we must beg the indulgence of our readers to admit a few more observations on the same topic.

It is not only from speculative researches, nor from discussions of abstract principles, nor from presenting petitions to parliament, that all the benefits from these societies can be hoped to be derived; neither can it be anticipated that if men could be instructed by them in most of the duties of life, they would necessarily become good men; but could a real interest be established in the members for moral truths, a desire to see them in practice would naturally follow, means would then probably be taken to encourage good conduct and to discountenance vice. It is true that no authority would exist in them to punish crimes, but the means of rewarding what should meet their approbation would rest with them; and should these societies find the support they seem to merit, the possession of their goodwill might become an object of no small importance to most men. In order then to promote good conduct, and to perform acts of individual benefit by the same proceeding, it might be first advisable for them to resolve:

That a subscription be formed for promoting such purposes, and for assisting such objects as may by the societies be judged proper; part of which subscription shall be applied in encouraging information of the good or bad conduct of persons within the district, parish, or county, as the case may be practicable. That a minute be made of the same, and preserved for a certain length of time in the societies' books; and that any one having within a stated period been guilty of certain offences, chiefly relating to *barbarity* exercised on persons or on dumb animals, shall be deemed incapable of receiving any benefit from the societies for such a period as may be thought fit. But where no such offence shall be proved, then part of the subscriptions shall go towards such cases as may appear most to need relief. For instance, in cases of poverty, sickness, want of employment, and to defray unjust law expenses which may have been incurred on such as may be unable to pay them by those who were; and part of the subscription should be employed for the benefit of animals, of those who had yielded their services to man and had become unfit for work.

The influence of these societies should be most extended to cases of guilt least cognizable by the law, and to such acts as are most opposed to natural morality. For instance, a person having committed an assault with extreme cruelty, should be considered more criminal than another who had committed a petty theft, though the law ordains the latter to suffer death, and the former to a milder sentence. The suppression of cruelty, and the amelioration of the state of brutes, in cases which might fail of engaging the attention of higher authority, should be two of the chief aims of these societies, affording a kind of negative redress where positive may be denied.

―――――

THOUGH perhaps misplaced, we cannot permit this opportunity to pass without adverting to an objection which has been made to Mr. Martin's proposed Amendment of this Bill. This gentleman has been taxed with interfering in the pastimes and diversions of the poor, by attempting to prevent the cruel sports of bull and bear baiting, etc., while the equally cruel sports of the rich of hunting and shooting have been passed over by him. But the absurdity of this charge is almost too evident to render a defence necessary. Does it follow that a person is to withhold the performance of the good which may be within his power, because he does not attempt that which may seem beyond it?   L.G.